Ang

by
Charles Capps
and
Annette Capps

Unless otherwise indicated, all Scripture quotations are taken from the *King James Version* of the Bible.

Some Scripture quotations marked AMP are taken from *The Amplified Bible, New Testament*. Copyright © 1954, 1958 by The Lockman Foundation, La Habra, California.

Some Scripture quotations marked AMP are taken from *The Amplified Bible, Old Testament*. Copyright © 1962, 1964 by Zondervan Publishing House, Grand Rapids, Michigan.

15 14 13   44 43 42

Angels
ISBN 13: 978-0-9819574-1-8
Formerly ISBN 10: 0-89274-308-5
Formerly ISBN 10: 0-89274-743-9
Revised © 1994 by Charles Capps
Copyright © 1984 by Charles Capps
P.O. Box 69
England, Arkansas 72046

Published by Capps Publishing
P.O. Box 69
England, AR 72046

Printed in the United States of America. All rights reserved under International Copyright Law. Contents and/or cover may not be reproduced in whole or in part in any form without the express written consent of the Publisher.

Contents

Introduction

We all have read of the ministry of angels, how throughout the Old Testament and even the New Testament they brought great deliverance to people and nations.

The Mosaic Law was given by the disposition of angels.

An angel appeared to Mary and told her she would conceive and bear a child.

The birth of Jesus in Bethlehem was proclaimed by angels.

Joseph was given direction several times. First, an angel told him not to fear, but to take Mary as his wife because that which was conceived in her was of the Holy Ghost. Then twice an angel appeared to him and told him where to go to avoid the people who were trying to kill Jesus.

It was great that the angels ministered to those people. But somehow down through the years we have let these things slip from us. We need to recognize that the ministry of angels didn't go out with the New Testament. It didn't go out with any dispensation. It's still a valid ministry in the earth today.

Hosea 4:6 says God's people are destroyed for lack of knowledge. But knowledge is available to us. Jesus said, "If ye continue in my word, then are ye my disciples indeed; and ye shall know the truth, and the truth shall make you free" (John 8:31,32).

There is a vast reservoir of knowledge concerning the ability of angels to deliver people from the bad circumstances of life, even from life and death situations. You can't believe any farther than you have knowledge.

It is my intention in this book to present an understanding of the ministry of angels as it is available to us today. With knowledge of angels and their work in the earth, we can better do the will of God which is the ultimate goal of every believer.

1
Angels, Good and Bad

I want us to begin in the first chapter of Hebrews, verses 4 and 7, where the writer is comparing Jesus with angels and His ministry with the ministry of angels.

> Being made so much better than the angels, as he hath by inheritance obtained a more excellent name than they.

> And of the angels he saith, Who maketh his angels spirits, and his ministers a flame of fire.

Then in verse 13:

> But to which of the angels said he at any time, Sit on my right hand, until I make thine enemies thy footstool?

We know He didn't say this to angels; He said it to Jesus!

> Are they not all ministering spirits, sent forth to minister for them who shall be heirs of salvation?
>
> Hebrews 1:14

The angels are spirits sent forth to minister for them who shall be heirs of salvation. That includes us!

So the ministry of angels didn't pass away with some other dispensation. It didn't stop when we entered into the New Testament. It didn't stop with the apostles. It's still a valid ministry today.

Fallen Angels

There are not only good angels, but there are fallen angels — angels that rebelled against God. It would be good for us to find out what the Bible says about these fallen angels.

One third of the angels fell from heaven with Lucifer when he rebelled against God. As a result they were cast out of heaven. (Rev. 12:9.) Let's look at Jude, the sixth verse:

> **And the angels which kept not their first estate, but left their own habitation, he hath reserved in everlasting chains under darkness unto the judgment of the great day.**

Notice these angels are reserved in everlasting chains under darkness.

Now in 2 Peter we find the angels that "kept not their first estate." They sinned, and lost their habitation. The Hebrew says "they kept not their first headship or first dominion."

> **For if God spared not the angels that sinned, but cast them down to hell, and delivered them into chains of darkness, to be reserved unto judgment;**
>
> **And spared not the old world, but saved Noah the eighth person, a preacher of righteousness, bringing in the flood upon the world of the ungodly.**
>
> 2 Peter 2:4,5

I want to draw your attention to one statement:

> **But cast them down to hell, and delivered them into chains of darkness to be reserved unto judgment;** *and spared not the old world....*

The world Satan (or Lucifer, as he was called then) ruled was a world ruled by angels. Lucifer ruled and reigned over a world before Adam was ever created. Lucifer had a throne; he ruled over

nations. The Bible doesn't give many details, but
it gives us some insight into that world. Let's read
Ezekiel 28:12-15:

> **Son of man, take up a lamentation upon
> the king of Tyrus, and say unto him, Thus saith
> the Lord God; Thou sealest up the sum, full of
> wisdom, and perfect in beauty.**

> **Thou hast been in Eden the garden of God;
> every precious stone was thy covering, the
> sardius, topaz, and the diamond, the beryl, the
> onyx, and the jasper, the sapphire, the emerald,
> and the carbuncle, and gold: the workmanship
> of thy tabrets and of thy pipes was prepared in
> thee in the day that thou wast created.**

> **Thou art the anointed cherub that
> covereth; and I have set thee so: thou wast upon
> the holy mountain of God; thou hast walked
> up and down in the midst of the stones of fire.**

> **Thou wast perfect in thy ways from the
> day that thou wast created, till iniquity was
> found in thee.**

Notice he said, "Thou art the anointed
cherub, and I have set thee so." This "being" he is
speaking of is Lucifer. The phrase, "Take up a

lamentation upon the king of Tyrus," is a double reference. The speaker is talking to a man on earth, but there is a dual reference which could not apply to a man on earth.

For instance, it says, "Thou hast been in Eden, the garden of God." It doesn't say, "the Garden of Eden." It says, "Eden, the garden of God." If you're not careful, you'll miss it there.

When Satan was in the Garden of Eden with Adam and Eve, he did not have diamonds and beryl and gold as his covering; he had a snakeskin! When the serpent started talking to Eve, she didn't say, "Oh, how beautiful and how shiny your diamonds are! My, my, your gold and your rubies are just out of this world!" She didn't say that because the covering of gold and rubies wasn't there when the serpent approached her. Satan had already fallen; he was already a fallen angel. He had lost all of his beauty before he was in the Garden of Eden. He lost it when he sinned against God. The Garden of Eden was *Adam's* garden!

Here it is called God's garden: "Eden, the garden of God." When Satan was in the Garden of God, all those precious stones were his covering. He was the anointed cherub. He was the protector of the earth and the ruler of that world. This is why the Bible speaks of "the old world" in 2 Peter 2:5.

Then in Isaiah, chapter 14, you will notice again some scriptures that give revelation concerning Lucifer. Verses 12-17 read:

> **How art thou fallen from heaven, O Lucifer, son of the morning! how art thou cut down to the ground, which didst weaken the nations!**
>
> **For thou hast said in thine heart, I will ascend into heaven, I will exalt my throne above the stars of God: I will sit also upon the mount of the congregation, in the sides of the north:**
>
> **I will ascend above the heights of the clouds; I will be like the most High.**
>
> **Yet thou shalt be brought down to hell, to the sides of the pit.**

> **They that see thee shall narrowly look
> upon thee, and consider thee, saying, Is this
> the man that made the earth to tremble, that
> did shake kingdoms; that made the world as a
> wilderness, and destroyed the cities thereof...”**

Notice he is talking about Lucifer, the anointed cherub. Lucifer had a throne. He ruled over people. Evidently, his throne was on earth because he said, "I'll exalt my throne above the stars of God." The stars were already there; they were already created. He said, "I'll ascend above the heights of the clouds," so the clouds were already there.

Lucifer had dominion. He had rule over a world, and all these precious stones were his covering. He was put there to be the anointed cherub. He ruled and reigned in that world.

Have you ever wondered why the statement was made in Hebrews 2:5:

> **For unto the angels hath he not put in
> subjection the world to come, whereof we speak?**

Why would he be talking about angels and suddenly make this statement: "The world to come will not be put into subjection to the angels"? Because *the world that was* had been in subjection to angels.

The world as we know it is not ruled by angels, but the angels have an important part here on earth, Hebrews 2:5,6 states:

> **For unto the angels hath he not put in subjection the world to come, whereof we speak.**
>
> **But one in a certain place testified, saying, What is man, that thou art mindful of him?**

I want to stress this point: Angels are created beings. We need to know the difference between angels and men, because there is much confusion in this area.

If you believe some of the things you see on television, you will think that when you die, you will become an angel. You're not an angel now, and you won't become an angel when you die.

No Salvation for Fallen Angels

There is no salvation for angels. I know there have been things taught concerning the restoration of all things, that even the devil himself is going to be saved! But you can forget it! The devil is not going to make it! He's had it!

This then brings up the question: Why would God give His Son for mankind and not for angels?

Like all angels, Lucifer was a created being. In the world that existed before Adam, angels ruled. Then when Adam was created, he was made ruler of the earth. He was subordinate to God, but he was "the god of this world." He had dominion and control over the earth. God gave him that dominion in Genesis 1:26-28.

First Peter 1:12 tells us that angels "desire to look into salvation." One reason there is no salvation for angels is that they are created beings. They were designed and set in a place to fulfill the purpose for which God created them. If they left their habitation or calling, it was curtains for them!

Angels must respond to what God has created them to do. They don't have the right to make choices. They have the *ability to choose* but not the *right of choice*.

The fallen angels didn't have the right to make the decisions that they made, but they made them anyway. Lucifer made a decision. He said, "I will exalt my throne!"

But the angels didn't have the right to speak their own words. They were to speak God's Word or things that were in line with God's Word. They were to enforce God's Word or see that it came to pass. They were to hearken to the Voice of God's Word. They were to do His commandments, but they chose to rebel against God.

Adam was created and put on the earth on a higher order than the angels. He had the ability and right to make decisions. God let His intentions be known by stating it this way:

> **Let us make man in our image, after our likeness: and *let them have dominion* over the fish of the sea, and over the fowl of the air, and over the cattle, and over all the earth, and over every creeping thing that creepeth upon the earth.**
>
> Genesis 1:26

God said, "We're going to give man dominion." Adam was created with the *ability of choice* and the *right of choice*. That's the reason God sent His Son: to redeem and restore mankind.

God created man on His level, in His image and likeness. He gave man dominion over the fish of the sea and the fowl of the air. He gave man total and complete dominion over all the earth.

Man could do what he wanted, but God told him, "You're going to die if you eat of the tree of knowledge of blessing and calamity!" (Gen. 2:17 AMP.)

Adam had the right to make the wrong choice. God gave him the right to do it, even though it was wrong. Adam shouldn't have done it, but he did!

God has always given man a choice. He gave man dominion over all the work of His hands.

God has laid out before us what's right and what's wrong. The choice is ours. We can choose right, or we can choose wrong.

God gave us His Word (the Bible) and said, "You have dominion. Sow the right seed and reap a good harvest."

The Word of God spells it out: Sow to the flesh, and you will of the flesh reap corruption. Sow to the Spirit, and you will of the Spirit reap everlasting life. (Gal. 6:8.)

Mankind is the only being with the right to choose his destiny. He is the only one that has the right to choose his words. Angels don't have that right.

God sent an angel to Cornelius and told him, "Go talk to Simon Peter, and he'll tell you what to do."

Why didn't the angel tell Cornelius what to do? **Angels can't preach the Gospel, but men can.** We were created on a higher order than angels. Demons, evil spirits, and fallen angels want mankind to believe they were created higher than man. The Apostle Paul said it this way:

> **For such are false apostles, deceitful workers, transforming themselves into the**

apostles of Christ. And no marvel; for Satan himself is transformed into an angel of light.

2 Corinthians 11:13,14

One translation reads, "Satan transforms himself into an angel of light."

Beware of satanic enlightenment.

God said, "Let us make man in our image and in our likeness (*likeness* indicates "a duplication of kind"), let them have dominion over the fish of the sea, over the fowl of the air, over all the earth, over every creeping thing that creepeth on the earth."

God gave man dominion over everything that *creepeth* on the earth! Yes, you have dominion over creeps!

So God created man in his own image, in the image of God created he him; male and female created he them.

And God blessed them, and God said unto them, Be fruitful, and multiply, and replenish the earth, and subdue it: and have dominion over the fish of the sea, and over the fowl of the

**air, and over every living thing that moveth
upon the earth.**

Genesis 1:27,28

Notice the word *dominion*: "Have *dominion*
over the earth." That word means "to rule," not
be subordinate to something else. Although
Adam was subordinate to God in the spirit realm,
he was the god of this world.

But after the Fall, Satan became the god of
this world. (2 Cor. 4:4.) Satan came into this
world illegally to force his rulership on this
planet, but God had given it to Adam. Where did
Satan get his title? He got it from Adam.

God had given man dominion. But He had
said to Adam:

> **Of every tree of the garden thou mayest
> freely eat: but of the tree of the knowledge of
> good and evil, thou shalt not eat of it: for in
> the day that thou eatest thereof thou shalt
> surely die.**

Genesis 2:16,17

God didn't say Adam *couldn't* eat of it. He said,
"You'll die if you do!" God had set Adam in this

earth in a different order than the angels in the world before, in that Adam had the right to choose. Adam was ruler, and he had dominion over the earth. It was his to do with what he would. He could eat or not eat of all trees in the Garden.

Allow me to paraphrase what God told Adam. "Now I'm telling you, Adam, in the same day that you eat the fruit of that one tree, you will die." The Hebrew says, "dying you shall die." Adam died spiritually at that moment, and his body began to die from that very day.

God created Adam a free moral agent with the right to make his own decisions. God gave him the earth lease. The Bible says:

> **The heaven, even the heavens, are the Lord's: but the earth hath he given to the children of men.**
>
> Psalm 115:16

Adam could do what he would with the earth, and he did. He sold the earth lease to Satan and left God on the outside.

Adam had the ability *and the right to make that decision.* Lucifer did not have such a right.

He had the *ability* to say, "I'll exalt my throne," but he didn't have the *right*. This is why there is no salvation for fallen angels.

> **For unto the angels hath he not put in subjection the world to come, whereof we speak.**
>
> **But one in a certain place testified, saying, What is man, that thou art mindful of him? or the son of man, that thou visitest him?**
>
> **Thou madest him a little lower than the angels; thou crownedst him with glory and honour, and didst set him over the works of thy hands (Hebrews 2:5-7).**

Now if words mean anything, this is saying that there was *nothing* that was not put under Adam's feet. That is not the situation with angels today.

Yet, it seems to contradict itself. Verse 7 says, "Thou madest him a *little lower than the angels.*" Then it begins to qualify this by saying he had dominion over everything and there was nothing that was not put under him. So that brings him up above angels.

Let's look at Psalm 8, which is the source of what Hebrews, chapter 2, related to us. Here is where it was taken from the Old Testament.

> **What is man, that thou art mindful of him? and the son of man, that thou visitest him?**
>
> **For thou hast made him a little lower than the angels, and hast crowned him with glory and honour.**
>
> **Thou madest him to have dominion over the works of thy hands: thou hast put all things under his feet.**
>
> Psalm 8:4-6

The Hebrew word translated *dominion* means "the right and power to govern and control." Then the Hebrew word translated *angels* in verse 5 is *Elohim,* which is plural for *God.*

It actually says, "Thou madest him a little lower than Elohim." Adam was created a little lower than God.

Now as you look at this statement, you might think I'm going a little too far with this. Well, as someone said, "Does anybody else believe it that way?" *There was a certain rabbi who believed it that way.* His name was Jesus. We find it in John 10:30-36:

> I and my Father are one.

> Then the Jews took up stones again to stone him.

> Jesus answered them, Many good works have I shewed you from my Father; for which of those works do ye stone me?

> The Jews answered him, saying, For a good work we stone thee not; but for blasphemy; and because that thou, being a man, makest thyself God.

> Jesus answered them, Is it not written in your law, I said, Ye are gods?

> If he called them gods, unto whom the word of God came, and the scripture cannot be broken; say ye of him, whom the Father hath sanctified, and sent into the world, Thou blasphemest; because I said, I am the Son of God?

Jesus was referring to Psalm 82:1.

> God standeth in the congregation of the mighty; he judgeth among the gods.

Three words in this one verse have the same meaning. The word translated God is Elohim, which is plural for God. It really says, *"Elohim standeth in the congregation of the Elohim; he judgeth among the Elohim."*

How long will ye judge unjustly, and accept the persons of the wicked? Selah.

Defend the poor and fatherless: do justice to the afflicted and needy.

Deliver the poor and needy: rid them out of the hand of the wicked.

They know not, neither will they understand; they walk on in darkness: all the foundations of the earth are out of course.

I have said, Ye are gods; and all of you are children of the most High.

But ye shall die like men, and fall like one of the princes.

Psalm 82:2-7

Jesus understood that man was created a little lower than God, not angels. This is the Old Testament scripture He is referring to in John

10:35 when He said, "I said, Ye are gods...unto whom the word of God came."

2
Fallen Angels and Giants

In this chapter we will deal with a subject that is somewhat controversial. It is not my intention to change the way you believe necessarily. However, regardless of your opinion or belief, you should hear the view that many Bible scholars take. Having heard, you can then make up your own mind.

The angels that did not keep their first estate, but left their own habitation, were cast down. They are now in hell, in chains of darkness, reserved unto judgment. There is a valid reason for this, and we find it in the Genesis account.

> And it came to pass, when men began to multiply on the face of the earth, and daughters were born unto them,
>
> That the sons of God saw the daughters of men that they were fair; and they took them wives of all which they chose.

And the Lord said, My spirit shall not always strive with man, for that he also is flesh: yet his days shall be an hundred and twenty years.

There were giants in the earth in those days; and also after that, *when the sons of God came in unto the daughters of men, and they bare children to them,* the same became mighty men which were of old, men of renown.

And God saw that the wickedness of man was great in the earth, and that every imagination of the thoughts of his heart was only evil continually.

And it repented the Lord that he had made man on the earth, and it grieved him at his heart.

Genesis 6:1-6

Then verse 8 says:

But Noah found grace in the eyes of the Lord.

I realize that there are two schools of thought concerning what I'm about to share. I'm just going to show you what I see in the Bible about it. You can believe the way you want. There were sons of God who left their habitation and took wives of the daughters of men.

Some say that "sons of God" doesn't mean angels, but rather sons of Seth.

There are only four scriptures in the Old Testament in which the expression "sons of God" is used: Genesis 6:1-4; Job 1:6; Job 2:1; Job 38:7. I believe all these scriptures refer to angels as sons of God. There is no disputing the fact that four of these refer to angels.

Nebuchadnezzar looked into the furnace and said, "I see One in there likened unto the Son of God." He was talking about an *angel of the Lord* that was in the furnace.

When God said, "the angel of the Lord," I believe that's exactly what He meant—His personal angel.

I believe all five of these Old Testament scriptures refer to angels. It says, "The sons of God came to the daughters of men." Some might argue that the Bible says angels are sexless, but I have not found any such statement in the Bible.

The Bible didn't say angels were sexless. Some have drawn that conclusion. The scripture that brings this conclusion to so many is Mark 12:25:

> **When they shall rise from the dead, they neither marry, nor are given in marriage; but are as the angels which are in heaven.**

We won't be operating in heaven as we are on earth because we will be as the angels. They are supernatural beings. We will have glorified bodies there.

From what the Scriptures say, many Bible scholars believe the angels that are now reserved in chains of darkness came to the daughters of men and produced a race of giants.

Ask yourself this question: **Where did the giants come from?** God's Law of Genesis says, *Everything produces after His and its kind.* Everything! When you plant a seed of cotton, you get cotton, not corn! People produce people. *Everything* reproduces after its kind.

A normal man and woman do not produce giants. If they did in the past, why not today? Many believe the giants' race began when angels came to the daughters of men. You can form your own opinion.

Og, king of Bashan, was a giant. His iron bedstead was eighteen feet nine inches long and eight feet four inches wide! (Deut. 3:11.)

Goliath evidently was about thirteen feet tall. He had a coat of mail that weighed 196 pounds.

There were nations of giants in those days. No wonder the children of Israel said, "We're like grasshoppers in their sight!" They were talking in the natural.

It is believed that Satan set out to pollute this earth and get rid of "the seed" that was to bring Jesus into the earth. It had to come from Adam's stock. When the Flood came upon the earth, Noah's was the only stock that hadn't been polluted. God preserved that lineage.

Again, after the Flood, the same thing happened, for it mentions in Genesis 6:4, "There were giants in the earth in those days" ("those days" being before the Flood). The phrase *after that* refers to after the flood. In other words, *before* and *after* the Flood.

This seemed to be Satan's plan to destroy the seed and keep Jesus from coming to the earth, for Jesus was the One Who was going to bruise Satan's head.

Satan was destined for destruction from Genesis 3:15 when God prophesied that **the seed of the woman would bruise the head** of the serpent. He tried every way he could to destroy the seed, but he failed.

This would explain why some things happened in the Bible that people didn't understand. Why did God tell Joshua to kill all the little children of Jericho? He said, "Kill all of the people when you go into this land." That included the little children because they were a polluted race! These scriptures in Genesis 6 indicate that fallen angels had come to earth and produced a race of giants. It was an evil race designed to destroy the pure stock (seed).

Delivered into Chains of Darkness

> ...God spared not the angels that sinned, but cast them down to hell, and delivered them into chains of darkness, to be reserved unto judgment; and spared not the old world, but saved Noah the eighth person....
>
> 2 Peter 2:4,5

This refers to several different periods of time and places. First, the Old World that passed away; then about Noah's flood; then the cities of Sodom and Gomorrah.

Jude picks up on this in verses 6 and 7:

> And the angels which kept not their first estate, but left their own habitation, he hath reserved in everlasting chains under darkness unto the judgment of the great day.
>
> Even as Sodom and Gomorrah, and the cities about them in like manner, giving themselves over to fornication, and going after strange flesh, are set forth for an example, suffering the vengeance of eternal fire.

Notice, not all fallen angels are reserved in chains. Only those that left their own habitation, *even as Sodom and Gomorrah, and the cities about them in like manner, giving themselves over to fornication....*

What is Jude talking about when he says *the angels* in like manner, giving themselves over to *fornication,* and going after *strange flesh?*

Josephus, the Jewish historian, made this statement: "Many angels of God accompanied and begat sons that proved unjust."

Then in Isaiah 26:13,14, there is an interesting note. In doing a study on the word *giants,* you find the *rephaim* that has been used in the Scriptures for giants. The word means "dead." It refers to *the dead that will rise not!* The giant race will not be raised up again. God has destroyed them.

3
Angelic Dominion Lost

For Christ also hath once suffered for sins, the just for the unjust, that he might bring us to God, being put to death in the flesh, but quickened by the Spirit:

By which also he went and preached unto the spirits in prison;

Which sometime were disobedient, when once the longsuffering of God waited in the days of Noah, while the ark was a preparing, wherein few, that is, eight souls were saved by water.

1 Peter 3:18-20

Personally, I could never understand how Jesus could preach to the wicked in prison. It was like giving them a second chance. But He *preached* to the spirits in prison. Evidently this is referring to the angels that kept not their first estate.

Hebrews 1:7 says, "And of the angels he saith, Who maketh his angels spirits, and his ministers a flame of fire." **He makes His angels spirits.**

Angels were created in a world before man. *Lucifer existed in a world before Adam.* When Lucifer came to the Garden of Eden, he was a fallen being. He had lost his throne. When he appeared on this earth he had already lost his dominion.

In the Garden of Eden he was not covered with diamonds, beryl, and gold. They had been stripped from him. He had lost it all in the Fall. He came to earth to deceive man and gain man's authority. And he did what he came to do! Adam sold the earth lease to Satan for the knowledge of evil.

There is a lease on this earth that runs for somewhere between six and seven thousand years. There can be no definite number of years put on it, for it depends on how long it takes the Body of Christ to put Satan under foot. But when that lease runs out, then Satan has had it, along with his demons and evil spirits!

I don't know or understand all the reasons why the evil spirits—the spirits of pre-Adamic creation—are not incarcerated now. But the demons understand that the day is coming when they will be. They challenged Jesus when He cast them out by saying, *"Have You come to torment us before the time?"* (Matt. 8:29.) They knew that a time was set. They thought Jesus couldn't cast them out before that time. One of them even had the audacity to say, "I adjure you by God that You torment me not!" (Mark 5:7.) He thought God would take up for him.

Seducing Spirits — Doctrines of Devils

Now the Spirit speaketh expressly, that in the latter times some shall depart from the faith, giving heed to seducing spirits, and doctrines of devils.

1 Timothy 4:1

Today, too many people are disturbed about demons and evil spirits. They are too demon and devil conscious, just as the Church in days past has been too sin conscious.

The devil wants to draw God's people away from the major things of the Word and over into a realm of dealing with the negative all the time.

If he can keep you busy dealing with evil spirits and all the things he is doing, you won't have time for what God is doing.

Some people think that demons are everywhere. Some of them go so far as to say that all Christians have demons and must be delivered.

Someone once asked me, "Do you believe in demons?"

I said, "No. I don't believe in demons. I believe there are demons, but *I don't believe in them. I believe in Jesus!*"

Certainly there are demons and demons do possess people at times; but Jesus didn't make a big deal out of it in His earthly ministry. He simply cast them out! The Bible says He cast them out with His Word!

The more attention you give to demons, the more they will manifest themselves. I have known people who thought there were demons under every rock and behind every door! Yes, there are demons; but when you know the Word of God and understand the power and authority that come with the name of Jesus, you cast them out.

As Paul said, some people will give heed to seducing spirits and doctrines of devils; *but it is time for the Body of Christ to begin to give heed to the spirits of God.* There are demons and there is a devil; but we have them outnumbered! As Elisha said, "There are more with us than there are with them!" Let's get turned on to the good spirits of God and not be so concerned about evil spirits.

I am not saying we should ignore those that need deliverance. But we don't have to spend all our time going on witch hunts or devil chases.

You can see the tactic of the devil in this. He is our enemy. His goal is to divert us from the ministering spirits of God.

Let's team up with God's Word and put our feet on the devil!

Quit testifying about what Satan is doing and *proclaim him to be a defeated foe.* Jesus fought him and won the victory for you. *Don't fight the battle again—just enforce his defeat.*

Don't put up with demons and evil spirits. Jesus said, "In My Name, cast out demons." You don't have to give heed to seducing spirits and doctrines of devils; make them give heed to you!

Get excited about angels and what they are doing today! Evil spirits are not ministering for you; they are against you. They are out to destroy you, but the name of Jesus will put them in their place!

> **Wherefore God also hath highly exalted him, and given him a name which is above every name:**
>
> **That at the name of Jesus every knee should bow, of things in heaven, and things in earth, and things under the earth.**
>
> Philippians 2:9,10

4
Angels and Supernatural Manifestations

by Annette Capps

When you are dealing with areas of the supernatural, such as the appearance of angels, people have a tendency to get excited. Very often, they have a difficult time keeping things in the right perspective and walking the straight and narrow path. They usually wind up going off into the ditch on one side or the other!

God has given me some instructions from His Word that will help keep us in the middle, in an area of balance. When you use the word "balance," some people's hair stands on end. They throw a fit! They think you are going to compromise the Word by mixing a little faith with a little suffering or unbelief. But that's not what I mean. It is the Word of God that will keep things in the right perspective.

As I travel around the country ministering God's Word, I see and hear lots of interesting things. I heard that in one particular church, there was a great stir over angels. Someone had seen a vision of an angel and, suddenly, everyone was excited and anxious to see angels.

One night during the service, the person directing it said, "Oh, angels are flying all around the congregation!" So everybody stood up and raised their hands, feeling for angels! One woman, who was kind of short, had her hands raised. When the man next to her moved his arm, her hand brushed his sleeve and she screamed, "I've got one!"

This a good example of people being overzealous about the supernatural. It shows what can happen when they don't have God's Word as a guide.

Supernatural manifestations will be more prominent in these days. Because of that, we need some guidelines to follow concerning revelations, visions, and angelic appearances.

First, you must understand that supernatural manifestations don't occur whenever you want them to. You can't just decide, "Today I'm going to have a vision," or, "Today I'm going to operate in the word of knowledge or the gift of prophecy." These things happen as the Spirit of God wills.

I have had several visions; but I wasn't sitting there saying, "Lord, I want a vision! Let me see an angel!" Each time it came as a surprise. I remember one of the first times I saw Jesus. I was ministering at a prayer meeting and had just finished praying for a lady. I saw someone walk up, so I turned to see who it was. It was Jesus! I no more expected to see Jesus than I expected to see an astronaut! But it wasn't as I chose it to be; it was as God willed.

Some people have had visions. Some have seen angels; some have seen Jesus. Others never have, and never will. That does not mean they are less spiritual. The Bible doesn't say, "Those who see angels and have visions are spiritually mature." Seeing visions does not mean you have more faith.

I don't know why God chooses to appear to certain people and not to others. If He appeared to some people, they would be like the little woman who screamed, "Wow! I've got one!".

Don't be concerned about seeing visions. Those things belong to God, and He will take care of it. If for some reason God wants Jesus to appear to you personally, then He will. If God wants you to see an angel, you will see one. Otherwise, don't be concerned about it.

How To Tell the Truth

People have said to me, "I hear one person say this and another say something else. How do I know truth from error?"

There are a few basic principles in God's Word which, if followed, will keep you from error. Always remember, you have the Spirit of Truth within you, and He will guide you into all the truth.

The Holy Spirit and angels do not have the same job. They operate in two different areas.

The Holy Spirit dwells *in* you. Angels do not dwell *in* you; they are here to minister *for* you.

John 14:26 tells us what the Holy Spirit does. Let's read from *The Amplified Bible:*

> **But the Comforter (Counselor, Helper, Intercessor, Advocate, Strengthener, Standby), the Holy Spirit, Whom the Father will send in My name [in My place, to represent Me and act on My behalf], He will teach you all things. And He will cause you to recall (will remind you of, bring to your remembrance) everything I have told you.**

The Holy Spirit is our Teacher. Angels do not operate in the office of teacher. They do not reveal the Word of God. They do not operate in revelation knowledge. That is the job of the Holy Spirit.

When the angel appeared to Cornelius in Acts, chapter 10, he didn't tell Cornelius the way of salvation. He didn't say, "Jesus Christ was the Son of God, come in the flesh. He came to save you, to redeem you." The angel simply said, "Send for a man named Peter."

Angels are not given responsibility of preaching or teaching God's Word. The Bible tells us that angels actually desire to look into things of salvation and redemption. (1 Pet. 1:10-12.) Evidently, they don't have revelation knowledge in that area. God is showing, through us, the wisdom of God to angels. (Eph. 3:10.) John 15:26 AMP says:

> **But when the Comforter (Counselor, Helper, Advocate, Intercessor, Strengthener, Standby) comes, Whom I will send to you from the Father, the Spirit of Truth Who comes (proceeds) from the Father, He [Himself] will testify regarding Me.**

Angels can and do comfort and help us; but they do it in the natural realm, often by moving circumstances in our favor or by causing supernatural manifestations of light, love, and comfort. The Holy Spirit is our Comforter and Helper, dwelling inside us and strengthening us from within our spirits.

John 16:13 AMP says:

> **But when He, the Spirit of Truth (the Truth-giving Spirit) comes, He will guide you**

into all the Truth (the whole, full Truth). **For He will not speak His own message [on His own authority] but He will tell whatever He hears [from the Father; He will give the message that has been given to Him]; and He will announce and declare to you the things that are to come [that will happen in the future].**

It is the job of the Holy Spirit to give you the truth. Romans 8:14 does not say, "As many as are led by *angels*, they are the sons of God." But, "As many as are led by the *Spirit of God*, they are the sons of God."

Occasionally, angels will be sent to give direction to individuals who are in unusually difficult circumstances. But the normal area of guidance will be the inward witness. Angels do, from time to time, give divine messages. They are often called messengers, but they do *not* bring revelation knowledge of God's Word.

Judge Appearance by God's Word

If an angel appeared and started trying to explain the Scriptures, I would be rather suspicious. Paul said there are many voices going out into the world, and none is without signification. (1 Cor. 14:10.)

There are many voices in the world today. If you are seeking after some great and mighty revelation that no one else has received, then you will probably get one. But it may be from the wrong source. There are many voices. There is the voice of people. There is the voice of God that comes through our spirits. There is also the voice of Satan. (He would be glad to give you a revelation!) If you seek after revelations or visions, you may open yourself to Satan, and he may give you satanic enlightenment.

Whenever you have a revelation, a vision, or a supposed appearance of an angel or even of Jesus, let peace be your guide. If you hear something that does not bring peace to your spirit and is not in line with God's Word, you can check it off your list because it is not of God.

As a general rule, angels do not reveal their names. The Scriptures do not forbid this, but we need to carefully try the spirits should this happen. There are only four angels in the Scriptures that are named. Two are evil: Lucifer and Abaddon (Apollyon). Two are good: Gabriel and Michael. There are many angels; but we do not have a book that tells us all about their names. There is a reason for that.

If God wanted us to know our guardian angel's name, He would have provided a book about angels that gives their names and how they appear; and there would be a continual revelation of angels' names. Obviously, there are some things God just does not want us to know.

Angels Unaware

When angels were seen as heavenly beings in the Bible, they always wore white. If an angel comes to you dressed in a black robe, he is probably not of God. There are what the Word calls "angels unaware." They would appear dressed as normal men. However, at the time, you would be unaware that you were in the presence of one of these supernatural beings.

In Galatians 1:6-9, Paul wrote:

I marvel that ye are so soon removed from him that called you into the grace of Christ unto another gospel: which is not another; but there be some that trouble you, and would pervert the gospel of Christ.

But though we, or an angel from heaven, preach any other gospel unto you than that which we have preached unto you, let him be accursed.

As we said before, so say I now again, If any man preach any other gospel unto you than that ye have received, let him be accursed.

This is pretty strong language. Paul doesn't say, "If any man disagrees with you on the minor doctrines and details of life, curse him! He is not talking about whether the church should have a small pulpit or a large pulpit, or how the chairs should be arranged! He is referring to people who try to pervert the Gospel of Christ by preaching some other doctrine or gospel.

Recognizing False Doctrine and Cults

How can you recognize people who are preaching other doctrines and gospels? Let's look in Colossians 2:18 AMP:

> Let no one defraud you by acting as an
> umpire and declaring you unworthy and
> disqualifying you for the prize, insisting on self-
> abasement and worship of angels, taking his
> stand on visions [he claims] he has seen, vainly
> puffed up by his sensuous notions and inflated
> by his unspiritual thoughts and fleshly conceit.

Self-Denial

A cult will have emphasis on self-denial.
There will be self-imposed fastings and self-
denial of many things in order to appear
religious. Cultists will deny themselves things
that are not forbidden in the Scriptures.

If the Spirit of God leads you to fast, and you
feel that you should, then follow that leading.
There are benefits from fasting, but you don't
have to go on forty-day fasts. Sometimes people
have caused themselves serious physical and
emotional problems because of long fasts.

The Word tells us that in the last days people
will forbid to marry and tell others to abstain
from meats. These areas of marriage and food

will become targets for Satan's deception. *Some people will overindulge, while others will deny themselves.* In order to get into the middle of the road, we have to hear what God is saying.

There have been people who have gone on a long fast and had a vision. They saw an angel that gave them a revelation. The only problem was that it was the wrong kind of angel. They were led off into error.

I think you will find in reading the Word of God that there were two instances of long fasts: Jesus went on a forty-day fast and afterwards He was ministered to by angels. Elijah went on the strength of what the angels fed him for forty days. Now if an angel came to me and fed me angelfood cake —*the real thing!* — I imagine I could go forty days, too! Daniel was on a partial fast for twenty-one days. Other than that, most of the fasts were no longer than three days, maybe a week.

When your body gets run down and you are weak and without strength, you open yourself to the enemy. When you are tired and worn out, when you haven't been eating right or sleeping enough, you have a tendency to get a little grouchy. You open yourself up to be critical. You yield yourself to the wrong spirit. (I don't mean that you are demon-possessed, but you do react a little bit below the level of God's love!)

Now just think about being on a forty-day fast. Unless you are really led by the Spirit of God, you are liable to get into trouble because you are not at your best; you are not on guard. This is why the devil will try to come at you in your sleep to try to harass you with fear. You are at rest then and not on guard mentally.

The same thing is true in this area of self-denial. If Satan can get you to go overboard, he can keep you from operating at your best. He will try to get at you any way he can. But, praise God, when you follow the Word, you will stay right in the middle of the road and not go off on one side or the other.

Worship of Angels

The word *worship* in Colossians 2:18 actually means "religion." So "worship of angels" would mean a "religion centered around angels," where there is an undue emphasis on either angels or demons.

You see, God wants to reveal His Word concerning angels so that He can operate at the fullest level supernaturally in the earth. But any time the Spirit of God desires to do something, the devil will try to counterfeit it.

The Spirit of God is endeavoring through teaching the Word on angels to allow us to tap into what God wants to do for us supernaturally. He wants to reveal to us that there are angels sent to minister for us and to us. Yet whenever the Spirit of God begins to give more revelation to the Body of Christ, then Satan usually comes right behind and brings in the counterfeit.

A cult will place undue emphasis on either angels or demons. But you have to get right in the middle of the road and say, "Yes, there are angels. I know my angels are out there working for me as I confess the Word. They hearken to the Word as it comes out my mouth. I know there are demons and evil spirits. But I have authority over them, in Jesus' name." You are not to put undue emphasis on the devil or on angels; you are to put your emphasis on Jesus!

You need to know what God's Word says specifically about angels. When you know what the Word says about angels, then you won't go off on a sideroad, always looking for angels. Keep everything in perspective. Worship Jesus and keep Him in the center of your thinking.

The problem comes when we take a truth and try to make it the truth. Yes, it is true that there are angels. They do work for us. Yes, it is true that there are demons. They work against us. Yes, it is true that we can have what we say. But if you take any one of those truths and try to make it the truth, you will be in error! Any time you place undue emphasis on one thing, you are out of line with the Word. If you are going to place all the emphasis on one thing, it had better be on Jesus because that is where the emphasis belongs!

Divine Visitations

A good way to recognize a cult is to realize that it is often based on a vision that was supposed to come from God or angels. If you study any cult, you will probably find that it began with some sort of supernatural visitation. Some had such great visitations and revelations, but they didn't agree with God's Word! There have been many such supernatural visitations in the Orient, but they don't agree with God's Word either!

Notice that Colossians 2:18 refers to "visions he claims he has seen." God will *not* have angels appearing to you or have you seeing some kind of vision just so you can say, "Hey, I'm spiritual! I had a vision! I saw an angel!"

The reason God would have an angel appear to you is to give you a message, or so that you would know you were protected in a dangerous situation, such as the case of Paul before his shipwreck. (Acts 27.)

If revelation knowledge is going to come forth in any vision or supernatural experience that God desires to give, then it will come without your seeking after it or looking for it. If you are always looking for supernatural appearances, then Satan may try to bring you satanic enlightenment.

Superior Knowledge

Many false religions are based on superior knowledge—new discoveries, a cult's secrets, and often piety and seeming to be religious, saying, "I've got a revelation that's better than yours." "Wait until you hear mine!"

Sometimes there are those who can share their revelation with only certain groups of people. They say, "God has revealed some things to me. I can't tell everybody about this great revelation because the Body of Christ at large wouldn't understand it; but I know that you are spiritually mature. You have the gifts, so I'm going to tell you about this."

Anything that is in the Word of God doesn't have to be withheld from the Body of Christ. We all have Bibles. Anything I say or any revelation I get should go right along with God's Word.

If you are looking for greater revelation, then your motive is not right, and it will cause you to get some kind of revelation that is definitely not of God.

Religion That Is Not Christ-Centered

True "religion" is Christ-centered and based on the truth of the Gospel of Jesus Christ. Its emphasis is not on visions, angels, and revelation. Its emphasis is on Jesus. The Spirit of God will always seek to uplift Jesus and magnify Him. It will not try to magnify men and make them look great.

You should always stay with the Word of God. Look to Jesus. We are going to see some supernatural things happening in the earth like never before. There will be more and more angelic appearances and supernatural manifestations. Just remember to keep your eyes on Jesus. Don't look at the visions. Don't base your faith on a vision, an angel, or a revelation. Base your faith on God's Word. Keep your relationship with the Lord Jesus Christ strong and firm.

5

Jesus and the Angels

As we begin this chapter, I want to lay a scriptural foundation from Hebrews, chapter 1, verses 1 through 14:

> God, who at sundry times and in divers manners spake in time past unto the fathers by the prophets,
>
> Hath in these last days spoken unto us by his Son, whom he hath appointed *heir of all things*, by whom also he made the worlds;
>
> Who being the brightness of his glory, and the express image of his person, and upholding all things by the word of his power, when he had by himself purged our sins, sat down on the right hand of the Majesty on high;
>
> *Being made so much better than the angels, as he hath by inheritance obtained a more excellent name than they.*
>
> *For unto which of the angels said he at any time, Thou art my Son,* this day have I begotten

thee? And again, I will be to him a Father, and he shall be to me a Son?

And again, when he bringeth in the first-begotten into the world, he saith, And let all the angels of God worship him.

And *of the angels he saith,* Who maketh his angels spirits, and his ministers a flame of fire.

But unto the Son he saith, Thy throne, O God, is for ever and ever: a sceptre of righteousness is the sceptre of thy kingdom.

Thou hast loved righteousness, and hated iniquity; therefore God, even thy God, hath anointed thee with the oil of gladness above thy fellows.

And, Thou, Lord, in the beginning hast laid the foundation of the earth; and the heavens are the works of thine hands: they shall perish; but thou remainest; and they all shall wax old as doth a garment;

And as a vesture shalt thou fold them up, *and they shall be changed: but thou art the same, and thy years shall not fail.*

But to which of the angels said he **at any time,** *Sit on my right hand,* **until I make thine enemies thy footstool?**

Are they not all ministering spirits, sent forth to minister for them who shall be heirs of salvation?

These verses of Scripture describe the ministry of Jesus. Jesus is the brightness of God's glory and the express image of God's person. He is the Word of God personified. "And the Word was made flesh, and dwelt among us" (John 1:14). There is no doubt that Jesus was the exact expression of God's Word in human form.

Once Jesus' identity is established, then the writer of Hebrews compares Him to angels.

Being made so much better than the angels, as he hath by inheritance obtained a more excellent name than they.

Hebrews 1:4

Jesus is greater than the angels —greater in power and in authority. He obtained His position by inheritance, by conquest, and it was bestowed upon Him. Because of His obedience, Jesus has been given the place of preeminence on the right hand of God. The angels, however, are our servants. They are ministering spirits that have been sent to minister for the heirs of salvation.

Ask yourself: Who are the heirs of salvation? Every born-again believer is an heir.

If ye be Christ's then are ye Abraham's seed, and heirs according to the promise.

Galatians 3:29

Good angels are supernatural beings sent to minister for us, to work for us, to do supernatural things that we can't do.

The night Jesus was taken captive at the Garden of Gethsemane, He said, "Don't you know that I can now pray and God will send more than twelve legions of angels?" (Matt. 26:53, paraphrased.) A Roman legion consisted of six thousand men. By praying one prayer, Jesus could have summoned 72,000 angels!

You might say, "Yeah, but He was the Son of God!"

Well, who do you think you are? "Beloved, now are we the sons of God" (1 John 3:2).

We have the ability as people born of God to summon the aid of angels. This is a part of our salvation.

6

Angels Ministering
for Heirs of the Promise

As we read from Hebrews 1:14 into the second chapter without stopping, you will notice that the subject matter does not change.

> **Are they not all (angels) ministering spirits, sent forth to minister for them who shall be heirs of salvation?**
>
> **Therefore we ought to give the more earnest heed to the things which we have heard, lest at any time we should let them slip.**
>
> Hebrews 1:14-2:1

What have we just heard? That the angels are ministering spirits sent forth in the earth to minister to the heirs of salvation. **We should give more earnest heed to that fact.**

> For if the word spoken by angels was stedfast, and every transgression and disobedience received a just recompence of reward;

> **How shall we escape, if we neglect so great**
> **salvation; which at the first began to be spoken**
> **by the Lord, and was confirmed unto us by**
> **them that heard him.**
>
> Hebrews 2:2,3

Notice the question in verse 3: "How shall we escape, if we neglect so great salvation?" We have always heard this scripture interpreted this way: "How are you going to escape hell if you neglect the salvation that Jesus has made available to us through His blood?" But this verse is not referring to being born again.

The word *salvation* here means "preservation, healing, soundness, and deliverance from temporal evils." This verse is referring not to our being born again, but to the deliverance that comes by the ministry of angels. How are you going to escape in this earth if you neglect the great deliverance that comes by supernatural beings called angels?

The ministry of angels is available to you. God provided this deliverance for you. But it is just like any other provision God has made:

Unless you believe it and act on it, you will not receive the full benefit of what is provided.

If you don't believe in the ministry of angels, you probably won't be bothered with them, even though they are here to minister for you.

You must believe in God's provision of ministering angels and allow them to work for you by cooperating with them and the Holy Spirit. The angels will get involved in your finances, your business affairs, and your family affairs.

While teaching on angels in a church in California, the spirit of prophecy came on me. I started saying some things prophetically about that church. Angels had been involved in their acquiring of the building. I heard myself say that the angels were not through, that they were going to become more involved in it because the people had released them. Then I pointed to the pastor and said, "There will be angels appear to you. You will see them, and they will talk with you."

My head gave me trouble over that. When the anointing left me, I thought, "Dear God, what did I say?"

Several months later the pastor told me that they were working on matters pertaining to the church and were having some severe problems. The pastor was in another city to hold a meeting. He was in a motel room, walking up and down, praying in the Spirit, getting ready for the service. He turned around, and there stood two angels dressed in armor and holding swords. The armor had marks on it like they had been doing battle. When he asked what they were doing there, they said, "We have come to help you with your church's financial matters if you tell us to." Well, it didn't take him long to tell them! He said, "Go, do it, in Jesus' name." And just like that, they were gone!

The next day he received a phone call from his church and learned that the problem which had been giving them so much trouble was all settled. Not long after that, a man called and said the Lord had directed him to give him 900 acres of land. They had a note due on that building. They had to come up with the money quickly, or they would lose everything. It was due on Monday and they needed over $300,000 more than they had. Sunday morning a fellow walked into the church and laid down two checks which added up to exactly the amount that they needed on Monday.

Somebody asks, "Why doesn't that ever happen to me?"

Have you ever believed for it? Have you ever said, "Ministering spirits, go and cause God's Word to be performed in my behalf"? We've let these things slip from us.

Ten Thousand May Fall, But You Won't

I will say of the Lord, He is my refuge and my fortress: my God; in him will I trust.

Thou shalt not be afraid for the terror by night; nor for the arrow that flieth by day;

Nor for the pestilence that walketh in darkness; nor for the destruction that wasteth at noonday.

**A thousand shall fall at thy side, and ten
thousand at thy right hand; but it shall not
come nigh thee.**

Psalm 91:2,5-7

Sometimes people will say, "I know what the
Bible says, but Brother So-and-so believed that
way and he got run over by a freight train."

I'm sorry about Brother So-and-so, but maybe
he didn't appropriate the promise. A person can
know about it and still not appropriate it.

They will say, "I know the scripture, but you
see So-and-so tried it that way, and he failed." As
Psalm 91:7 says, "A thousand shall fall at thy side,
and ten thousand at thy right hand...."

You could give me the names and addresses of
9,999 more that failed the same way, but it still
won't come nigh me! God has given His angels
charge over me, and they keep me in all my ways!

Just say what God said about it. You can't tell
how other people believe. You can't always tell
where they missed it. But God's Word didn't fail.

**Only with thine eyes shalt thou behold
and see the reward of the wicked.**

Because thou hast made the Lord, which is my refuge, even the most High, thy habitation; there shall no evil befall thee, neither shall any plague come nigh thy dwelling.

For he shall give his angels charge over thee, to keep thee in all thy ways.

They shall bear thee up in their hands, lest thou dash thy foot against a stone.

Because he hath set his love upon me, therefore will I deliver him: I will set him on high, because he hath known my name.

Psalm 91:8-12,14

God will set you on high because you know His Name.

There are too many Christians who don't know God's Name. They don't know God is El Shaddai—the all-sufficient God, the God Who is more than enough. He is El Shaddai, not El Cheapo! He is Jehovah-Rapha, the Lord that healeth thee, but so many don't know His Name. They don't know Him as Jehovah-Rapha.

> **He shall call upon me, and I will answer
> him: I will be with him in trouble; *I will deliver
> him,* and honour him.**
>
> **With long life will I satisfy him, and shew
> him my *salvation.***

Psalm 91:15,16

The word *salvation* in Romans 10:9 and Hebrews 2:3 means "preservation, healing, soundness, and especially deliverance from temporal evils."

How shall we escape if we neglect the deliverance that comes by the ministry of angels? The ministry of angels is part of the salvation that God has provided for you. It's foolish to partake of part of it and not partake of the other part. There are Christians all over the world who partake of the new birth, but don't believe in healing. Others believe in healing and the new birth, but don't believe in prosperity. Second Peter 1:3 says, "He has given us all things that pertain unto life and godliness." He's already given it! But you must believe for it.

Part of the salvation or deliverance that God has made available to us comes by the ministry of angels. "With long life will I satisfy him, and shew him my salvation."

Angels want very much to get involved in your physical affairs—in your home, in your business, in every affair of your life. The ministering spirits of God are here in the earth to work for *you!*

7
Angels Are Listening

As I was praying one day, the Spirit of God began to speak to my spirit. He shared some things with me about angels and how they operate in our behalf. He said:

> You have been wanting to know about confession and why it works. You have been practicing the Word and putting it into motion. You have been saying what My Word says. Now I am going to share with you why it works.

> One reason the words you speak are so important is because the angels are listening to what you say. People think I tell the angels what to do; but most of the time you are the one who gives them their assignment.

> I designed them as ministering spirits. They stand beside you daily, listening to the words that come out of your mouth. If your words are in line with My Word, then the angels go to work immediately, causing the things you speak to come to pass. But if you

speak things that are contrary to My Word, you won't get an audience with angels. They won't operate on those words.

Words spoken contrary to My Word will bind the angels. They will back off, fold their hands, and bow their heads. They are bound. They are designed as ministering spirits to minister *for you*. They listen to *your* voice, to *your* words. My Word is My will for man. You should always speak in line with My Word in order for My will to come to pass in your life. Man was designed to speak truth, to speak His will.

Then I remembered the words of Jesus in Matthew 5:37. He said, "Let your communication be, Yea, yea; Nay, nay: for whatsoever is more than these cometh of evil." Jesus taught that man should speak his will and not bring foolish words into the conversation. Again, the words of Jesus ring clear in Matthew 12:34-37.

Out of the abundance of the heart the mouth speaketh. A good man out of the good treasure of the heart bringeth forth good things: and an evil man out of the evil treasure bringeth forth evil things.

But I say unto you, That every idle word that men shall speak, they shall give account thereof in the day of judgment.

For by thy words thou shalt be justified, and by thy words thou shalt be condemned.

Idle Words—Non-Working

We will give account of every idle word that we speak. In the Greek text, *idle* means "non-working." We will be held accountable for the words that don't work for us. Jesus placed great importance on the words that come out our mouths, because the words that come out our mouths get into our spirits (hearts).

In Romans 10:8, Paul wrote:

But what saith it (the righteousness which is of faith)? The word is nigh thee, even in thy mouth, and in thy heart: that is, the word of faith, which we preach.

He said that *word is in your mouth first, then in your heart*.

Deuteronomy 30:14 says:

> **But the word is very nigh unto thee, in thy mouth, and in thy heart, that thou mayest do it.**

As you speak words, they are carried down into your inner being (your spirit).

Jesus' statement in Matthew 12:37 shows the vital importance of words:

> **For by thy words thou shalt be justified, and by thy words thou shalt be condemned.**

If words are that important, they must be doing something! They are not only working for you on the outside, communicating your thoughts to others; they are also working on the inside, building an image in your spirit. *"Where there is no vision, the people perish. As in water face answereth to face, so the heart of man to man"* (Prov. 29:18; 27:19).

Images are put into your spirit by words. **Words produce images.**

Angels are listening to your words, so the words you speak should be your will. You were designed in the likeness of God, in His image. You shouldn't speak words that are not your will.

The way you get angels involved in the affairs of your life is by keeping your words in line with God's Word. **The answer to most of your problems is found one inch below your nose: your mouth!** The key to prosperity and success in every area of life is to keep God's Word in your mouth. God said to Joshua:

> **This book of the law shall not depart out of thy mouth; but thou shalt meditate therein day and night, that thou mayest observe to do according to all that is written therein: for then thou shalt make thy way prosperous, and then thou shalt have good success.**

> Joshua 1:8

This is where most people run into problems. They let the Word depart out of their mouth, or they really never put it in their mouth. They may talk the right way for a while, but when things go wrong, they say, "Why me, Lord? I don't know why God allowed this to happen. I just don't understand. It must not be God's will." They talk doubt, fear, and unbelief; and they bind their angels from working in their behalf.

Forget None of His Benefits

Notice Psalm 103:1,2:

> **Bless the Lord, O my soul: and all that is
> within me, bless his holy name. Bless the Lord,
> O my soul, and forget not all his benefits.**

Do you realize what this is saying? Don't
forget any of His benefits. **The angels are a part
of His benefits**, and we have forgotten them.
We have let these things slip from us. We say,
"Well, when we get to heaven, everything will
work out all right." Yes, things will work out fine
when we are in heaven. But if we learn to
cooperate with our angels, **things will work out
here on earth also!**

God designed the angels to hearken to the
voice of His Word. If you will get your mouth
straightened out and your mind renewed to the
Word of God, you will see many of the things
come to pass on earth that you thought would
only happen in heaven.

You need the supernatural beings of God working for you here on earth. Begin to use all that God has made available to you.

Kingdom Rules Over All

The Lord hath prepared his throne in the heavens; and his kingdom ruleth over all.

Psalm 103:19

His throne is in heaven, but His Kingdom rules over all! According to Luke 12:32, the Father gave us the Kingdom. But where is the Kingdom? Jesus said the Kingdom of God is within you. (Luke 17:21.)

Out of the Abundance of the Heart the Mouth Speaketh

From your inner man come spirit words which either bring to pass or nullify God's will in your life. Jesus said:

The words that I speak unto you, they are spirit, and they are life.

John 6:63

This is why confession is so vital. The only way you will ever be able to operate in spirit words the way Jesus and the apostles did is to keep them in your mouth: **Speak God's Word.** You have to put God's Word into your spirit by speaking it until those words come forth from you without hesitation.

At the Gate Beautiful, Peter spoke spirit words to the lame man. Out of his spirit came words of life:

> **Such as I have give I thee: In the name of Jesus Christ of Nazareth rise up and walk.**
>
> Acts 3:6

The Kingdom that is within you has all the power and ability of heaven behind it. Jesus said:

> **If a man love me, he will keep my words: and my Father will love him, and we will come unto him, and make our abode with him.**
>
> John 14:23

Then in John 15:7, He said:

> **If ye abide in me, and my words abide in you, ye shall ask what ye will, and it shall be done unto you.**

Paul wrote:

> **Let no corrupt communication proceed
> out of your mouth, but that which is good to
> the use of edifying, that it may minister grace
> unto the hearers. And grieve not the holy
> Spirit of God, whereby ye are sealed unto the
> day of redemption.**
>
> Ephesians 4:29,30

It grieves the Spirit of God when you bind your angels. Words will bind and words will loose; **you** are the one doing the binding and loosing. The sooner you realize this, the sooner you will be on your way to victory.

Power of Binding and Loosing

Without your cooperation, your angels are bound. Your words of doubt and unbelief will bind your angels.

Jesus spoke of this in Matthew 16:19 when He said:

> **And I will give unto thee the keys of the
> kingdom of heaven; and whatsoever thou shalt**

**bind on earth shall be bound in heaven: and
whatsoever thou shalt loose on earth shall be
loosed in heaven.**

The Amplified Bible says it this way:

**I will give you the keys of the kingdom of
heaven, and whatever you bind (declare to be
improper and unlawful) on earth must be what
is already bound in heaven; and whatever you
loose (declare lawful) on earth must be what is
already loosed in heaven.**

It is the will of God for the earth to be like
heaven. Just ask yourself, "What is it that is
bound out of heaven?"

The power of binding and loosing is on earth,
not in heaven. If you choose to loose angels, all
heaven will stand behind you. You have the right
to do so. But you can bind them by only a few
words of unbelief.

One translation says, "Whatever you bind on
earth, whatever you have authority to bind on
earth, is what is already bound in heaven. What
you have authority to loose on earth is already
loosed in heaven."

What is bound out of heaven? Poverty, sickness, trouble, pain, strife, confusion, and every evil work. None of these things are found in heaven, so you have the authority to bind these things on earth. You won't be able to bind them off the whole earth; but by developing your faith in God's promises, you can bind them off the part that you walk on!

Accounting for Idle Words

The angels are on your side. They want to work for you. They are interested in your welfare. They are designed of God to do that. *But whatever you bind will be bound; whatever you loose will be loosed.* Ministering spirits can be bound or loosed by your words. You can lose reward or gain reward by the words that you speak. Jesus said you will give account of *every idle word.*

Some of you loose words with your mouth and destroy the work of the angels in your behalf. Then you cry out, "Dear God, why did You let this happen to me?" Don't blame God. You are the one that set it in motion. You have the choice: You can speak faith-filled words and put the angels to work for you; or you can speak fear-filled words and stop them.

Many times we have said things in the presence of an angel that has bound him when we were in a desperate situation. God could have been just on the verge of manifesting what we had confessed. The angel was just about to bring it into manifestation when he heard us say, "Well, it's just not working out. It always happens this way. Nothing ever works out for me. I guess it must not be God's will."

Be careful what you say! Your angels are listening!

Don't speak negative words before your angels. When the enemy comes in, like a flood the Spirit of God shall raise up a standard against him. (Isa. 59:19.) Get that standard raised up with the words of your mouth. Your angels are listening. They hearken to the voice of God's Word that comes out of your mouth.

Many a deal has been lost through negative confession. Many a businessman has gone bankrupt because of the words of his mouth.

Negative words will deceive the heart. The heart produces what is put in it by your words. If you talk defeat, then defeat will be produced. When you speak words of defeat, you not only bind your angels from working for you, but you send your voice into your heart and plant seeds of defeat.

"Nothing I ever do works out."

"I'll never have anything."

"I'll never get healed."

These phrases are seeds you are sowing. When you say these things, your heart (spirit) works day and night to bring them to pass. The heart doesn't decide if the words are good, bad, or indifferent. The human spirit was designed by God to produce or lead you to what you speak. Just because you say it once or twice does not mean it will come to pass. It comes to pass after it is spoken over a period of time.

When people hear someone preaching about confessing the Word for healing, they sometimes get all excited and decide to jump on the bandwagon. They say, "I think I'll try that." Then a couple of times they proclaim: "I believe I'm healed." When the manifestation doesn't come immediately, they say, "Oh, that's a bunch of nonsense! Confession doesn't work for me!"

Yes, it works. It began working the moment they said that, only it worked *against* them rather than *for* them. They said it didn't work, and it didn't. *The confession principle does not work just because you say it, but saying it is involved in working the principle.*

Also I say unto you, Whosoever shall confess me before men, him shall the Son of man also confess before the angels of God:

But he that denieth me before men shall be denied before the angels of God.

Luke 12:8,9

This is Jesus talking. His words are truth. If Jesus said it, you can believe it. How do you put the angels to work? By confessing Jesus before men. Stop and think for a moment: Who is Jesus? According to John 1:14 Jesus is *the Word of God personified*. When you confess the Word, you are confessing Jesus. You cannot separate Jesus from the Word.

Jesus was saying, "If you confess *My Word* (Me) before men, then I will confess you before the angels of God." In other words, "I will give you an audience before the angels of God."

"But he that denieth me before men shall be denied before the angels of God." If you deny Jesus (the Word), you will be denied an audience with the angels, even though the angels of God are here and available to minister for you.

The angels are governed by the precepts of the Supreme Court of the Universe, which is the Word of God. Their job is to do what God assigns them to do. As you speak God's Word in faith with your own mouth, you commission the angels to move according to that Word.

Your angels are listening! Learn to speak the Word of God with your own mouth. Put it to work for you. When you do, you will begin to see God's Word come alive in your life. You will get your angels involved.

It is not within your power as a human being to command angels to do anything you want them to do. But according to the Word of God, they are listening to what you say. Your words do, however, determine to a great extent what the angels can do in your behalf.

You have a physical body which gives you legal authority in the earth to destroy, loosen, dissolve, and undo the works of the devil. Angels do not have physical bodies as we have. Though they can take a physical form at times, they do not have the authority of man. *You* have legal authority here. *You* have legal authority to call upon these ministering spirits to work in your behalf. But they must have your cooperation. **They are waiting for you to speak God's Word.**

Some of you have problems beyond what you think anybody could solve, but learn to loose your angels. Let them work for you.

Putting Angels to Work

How do you put the angels to work for you? There are two ways: by prayer or by speaking God's Word in faith. The angels are listening to your words. God does not always tell them what to do. You are also voicing their assignment. You should not pray to angels, but you can pray for God to send angels in your behalf if you keep His Word.

Hebrews 2:3 states, "How shall we escape, if we neglect so great salvation?" How are you going to escape trials, tests, troubles, problems of life, and persecution if you neglect so great a deliverance that angels bring? The angels have been sent to minster for you. How are you going to escape if you neglect their ministry?

There is supernatural deliverance available to you through the ministry of angels. Don't let your angels stand idle. Put them to work. They are listening to your words.

Words and No Voice

Bless the Lord, ye his angels, that excel in strength, that do his commandments, hearkening unto the voice of his word.

Psalm 103:20

What is the *voice* of God's Word? We know that the Bible is the Word of God. But you can hold a Bible to your ear and not hear a thing! God's Word in written form makes no sound. It has no voice by itself. *It is God's Word, but there is no sound until you give voice to it. You must give voice to God's Word! Angels hearken to that sound.*

Just because the Bible says, "By His stripes, ye were healed," does not mean you will receive the benefits of it. It won't work just because you read it in the Bible. It won't work just because you believe the Bible is true. It will work only when you get that Word down in your spirit and give voice to it.

When people talk contrary to God's Word, the angels hear, back off, and fold their hands. **They can't work because they hearken to the voice of God's Word.**

How are angels going to hear the voice of His Word if you don't speak it? They can't act in your behalf when they hear words like, "It's not working out. We will never get our debts paid. I'll never have the money to make the payment on this car. You just watch, we'll lose our car!"

This person is not voicing God's Word. He is voicing the word of the enemy. By speaking those words of unbelief, he is binding and provoking the angels. Not only that, he has loosed Satan to operate with those words.

You Furnish the Voice for God's Word

What do angels do? They do God's commandments.

> **Bless the Lord, ye his angels, that excel in strength, that do his commandments....**
>
> Psalm 103:20

How do they do His commandments? By "hearkening unto the voice of His Word." Angels hearken, listen, and become obedient to the voice of God's Word. They actually work to cause God's Word to come to pass.

If *you* don't give God's Word a voice, then the angels have no voice to hearken to in the earth. The power of binding and loosing is on earth. This is where many of God's people miss it. They are not giving voice to His Word.

Bless ye the Lord, all ye his hosts; ye ministers of his, that do his pleasure.

Psalm 103:21

Who are the "minsters of his"? They are the ministering spirits who have been sent forth to minister for the heirs of salvation.

What do they do? This verse says they "do his pleasure."

What is the pleasure of the Lord? That His Word be fulfilled.

If God desires that His Word be fulfilled and if the angels are to do His pleasure, then they will cause His Word to come to pass. I found this secret several years ago, and it ministered to me. God's Word will put you over if you are obedient to it. When you speak it, the angels go to work, bringing it to pass in your behalf.

Hebrews 4:12 describes the Word of God as quick, powerful, and sharper than any two-edged sword. It will deliver you from the bondage of the evil one.

Jesus said:

> **Out of the abundance of the heart the mouth speaketh. A good man out of the good treasure of his heart bringeth forth good things: and an evil man out of the evil treasure of his heart bringeth forth evil things.**
>
> Matthew 12:34,35

If you don't have the good things of God's Word in your heart, you will be unable to bring forth those good things. You have to get God's Word in your heart and say what God says about you.

The angels are waiting for you to say things that will loose them! Begin to speak the Word of God. **Loose your angels!** Proclaim the mountain is removed from your life. Say, "I proclaim, in Jesus' name, that the mountain is removed! The mountain of financial adversity is removed!" You speak to the problem and tell it what to do.

Are you a giver? Luke 6:38 says, "Give, and it shall be given unto you." If you are a giver, then you can boldly say, "Yes, I'm a giver, so it is given unto me because I am obedient to God's Word." You can actually speak in the past tense. As far as God and His Word are concerned, it has already been given to you.

I don't care what the devil tries to tell you. You can stand your ground, shake your fist in his face, and say:

"No, Satan! In the name of Jesus, God's Word says when I give, it shall be given unto me. I am a giver. I have been obedient, and I refuse to allow you to rob me of what is mine. I demand my rights. I'm saying what God's Word says. I say in the name of Jesus that I have abundance. There is no lack. My God meets my need according to His riches in glory by Christ Jesus. I'll not fail for the Word of God shall never fail. Jesus has been made unto me wisdom, righteousness, sanctification, and redemption. Therefore, I have the mind of Christ. The wisdom of God is formed within me."

Things may look their darkest, but don't be moved by the circumstances. Begin to voice God's Word. Begin to speak it. Keep God's Word in your mouth.

You have God, His Word, and the angelic host of heaven on your side. When God is for you, who can successfully be your enemy?

Angels are very much alive and well in the earth. They worked in Old Testament times. They work in New Testament times. If you will give voice to God's Word, they will work for you today! **Don't provoke your angels— release them!**

8

Don't Provoke Angels

In Exodus 23:20-23 God said to Israel:

> Behold, I send an Angel before thee, to keep thee in the way, and to bring thee into the place which I have prepared.

> Beware of him, and obey his voice, provoke him not; for he will not pardon your transgressions: for my name is in him.

> But if thou shalt indeed obey his voice, and do all that I speak; then I will be an enemy unto thine enemies, and an adversary unto thine adversaries.

> For mine Angel shall go before thee, and bring thee in unto the Amorites, and the Hittites, and the Perizzites, and the Canaanites, the Hivites, and the Jebusites: and I will cut them off.

Notice God said, "An **Angel** will go before thee and bring thee to the place."

The place that God had prepared was the Land of Promise, the land that flowed with milk and honey. He said, "I've assigned an angel to bring you to the place that I've prepared for you. It's My will that you go there. I've already given the land to you. It belongs to you. It's yours and I've assigned a special angel to keep you in the way while you're going and bring you to the place that I have given you." Canaanland, the Land of Promise that flowed with milk and honey, was God's will for Israel, and He had assigned an angel to make sure they made it there.

Yet, thousands of them died in the wilderness and never made it to the Land of Promise. Everyone from twenty years of age and older died in the wilderness over a forty-year period because they wouldn't believe God and accept the direction of the Angel. They murmured and complained against God. **They provoked the angel that God has assigned to them.**

God had warned them, "Beware of him. Obey his voice. Provoke him not, for he will not pardon your transgressions for My name is in him." God wasn't talking about personal sins, but about provoking an angel.

An angel won't forgive you if you provoke him. He is not human. He doesn't have to forgive. In other words, God is saying that you will reap a just recompense of reward for what you speak.

In Numbers 14:28 God told the children of Israel, "I will do (allow to come to you) everything you **speak** in My ear. Whatever you say in My ear is what is going to happen to you."

What had they been saying? "Would to God that we'd stayed in Egypt! We're all going to die here in the wilderness!" Then snakes came among them, and they died by the thousands.

Why? Was it God's will? Certainly not! It couldn't have been. He had already assigned an angel to keep them in the way and bring them to the place that He prepared for them. But they provoked the angel, and he wouldn't forgive them. The words they spoke out of their own mouths came to pass. They called it forth with their own voice, and God got all the blame for it. Yet it wasn't God at all. God had told them, "This is the way it works. Whatever you say is what's going to happen. What you say is what you get." And they said, "We're all going to die." They provoked an angel. Many of them died in the wilderness, even though God had provided supernatural deliverance.

The third and fourth chapters of Hebrews explain very clearly what happened in the wilderness:

> **Wherefore (as the Holy Ghost saith, To day if ye will hear his voice, harden not your hearts, as in the provocation, in the day of temptation in the wilderness: When your fathers tempted me, proved me, and saw my works forty years.**
>
> **Wherefore I was grieved with that generation, and said, They do alway err in their heart; and they have not known my ways.**
>
> **So I sware in my wrath, They shall not enter into my rest.)**
>
> **Take heed, brethren, lest there be in any of you an evil heart of unbelief, in departing from the living God.**
>
> **But exhort one another daily, while it is called To day; lest any of you be hardened through the deceitfulness of sin.**

For we are made partakers of Christ, if we hold the beginning of our confidence stedfast unto the end;

While it is said, To day if ye will hear his voice, harden not your hearts, as in the provocation.

For some, when they had heard, did provoke: howbeit not all that came out of Egypt by Moses.

But with whom was he grieved forty years? was it not with them that had sinned, whose carcases fell in the wilderness?

And to whom sware he that they should not enter into his rest, but to them that believed not?

So we see that they could not enter in because of unbelief.

Let us therefore fear, lest, a promise being left us of entering into his rest, any of you should seem to come short of it.

For unto us was the gospel preached, as well as unto them: but the word preached did not profit them, not being mixed with faith in them that heard it.

Hebrews 3:7-19; 4:1,2

This is what provoked the angel: **They heard what God said, but they didn't mix faith with it.** They refused to believe God. They complained and said, "We are all going to die out here in this wilderness!" And they did! They provoked their angel and they received a just recompense of reward. They received the results of what they said.

People talk about "wilderness experiences" and claim that those experiences make them stronger; but it didn't work that way for the Israelites. Their wilderness experience didn't make them stronger; **it killed them!** We should take heed to this and make sure that we don't provoke our angel concerning the promises of God.

The Promised Land to us today is the promises found in the New Covenant. Canaanland was not a type of heaven. It couldn't have been because there were enemies there and wars to be fought. The Promised Land was a type of your inheritance in this life.

If you are to enter into it, you must believe and act on God's Word. You won't be healed by the stripes of Jesus just because the Bible says, "By His stripes ye were healed." You must actively believe and act on it. If God assigned an angel to Israel to bring them to their Promised Land, I believe He has assigned angels to the Church (the Body of Christ), to bring us to the place that He has prepared for us. God is not a respecter of persons.

God has assigned angels to the Body of Christ to bring us into the fullness of the New Covenant. But His instructions to the children of Israel apply to us as well: "Obey his voice and provoke him not." If we provoke angels, they will not let us off, but we will receive a just recompense of reward.

It is better not to speak at all than to speak doubt. When God has spoken, who are we to speak contrary to what He has established?

Let the words of my mouth, and the meditation of my heart, be acceptable in thy sight, O Lord, my strength, and my redeemer.

Psalm 19:14

Lot's Wife Provoked Angel

Throughout the Old Testament, we find angels ministering to the needs of God's people.

Genesis, chapter 19, tells the story of Sodom and Gomorrah. Angels played an important role in this act of judgment. Here again we see the results when angels are provoked.

> **And when the morning arose, then the angels hastened Lot, saying, Arise, take thy wife, and thy two daughters, which are here; lest thou be consumed in the iniquity of the city.**

> **And while he lingered, the men laid hold upon his hand, and upon the hand of his wife, and upon the hand of his two daughters; the Lord being merciful unto him: and they brought him forth, and set him without the city.**

> **And it came to pass, when they had brought them forth abroad, that he said, Escape for thy life; *look not behind thee*, neither stay thou in all the plain; escape to the mountain, lest thou be consumed.**

> Genesis 19:15-17

But Lot pleaded with them to let him flee to a nearby city rather than to the mountains. The angel said:

> **I have accepted thee concerning this thing also, that I will not overthrow this city, for the which thou hast spoken. Haste thee, escape thither; for I cannot do any thing till thou be come thither.**
>
> **The sun was risen upon the earth when Lot entered into Zoar.**
>
> **Then the Lord rained upon Sodom and Gomorrah brimstone and fire from the Lord out of heaven;**
>
> **And he overthrew those cities, and all the plain, and all the inhabitants of the cities, and that which grew upon the ground.**
>
> **But his wife looked back from behind him, and she became a pillar of salt.**
>
> Genesis 19: 21-26

The two angels came to deliver Lot and his family before the city of Sodom was destroyed. Notice that the word spoken by the angel was steadfast: Everything the angel said came to pass just as he said it would. He instructed them to flee and not look behind them. But Lot's wife disobeyed. When she looked back, she turned into a pillar of salt. The word of the angel was steadfast. Lot's wife provoked the angel, and she received the just recompense of reward.

In Luke's gospel, Jesus said:

> **But the same day that Lot went out of Sodom it rained fire and brimstone from heaven, and destroyed them all.**
>
> **Even thus shall it be in the day when the Son of man is revealed.**
>
> **In that day, he which shall be upon the housetop, and his stuff in the house, let him not come down to take it away: and he that is in the field, let him likewise not return back.**
>
> *Remember Lot's wife.*
>
> Luke 17:29-32

Jesus is talking about the end time. Notice His words in verse 32: *Remember Lot's wife.* That's the whole verse. That's all He says about it. He's talking about the end time when the Son of Man shall be revealed, and He says, *Remember Lot's wife.*

Why would He make such a statement here in this context?

He had just said, "So as it was in the days of Sodom and Gomorrah when Lot came out of Sodom, so shall destruction come the same day we leave the earth." Angels are going to play an important part in directing us in this day. We must be sensitive to the ministry of angels. According to Scripture they give direction in life when the heat is on. Take heed that you don't let these things slip from you. An angel appeared to Paul and told him how to save the lives of all the people on the ship.

When you start believing in the ministry of angels, you will have more manifestation of their ministry. But don't go *trying* to get angels to appear to you. Just believe the Word of God and believe for the supernatural ministry to come as you need it.

Zacharias Provoked Angel

In the first chapter of Luke we find another account of an angel being provoked.

And there appeared unto him (Zacharias) an angel of the Lord standing on the right side of the altar of incense. And when Zacharias saw him, he was troubled, and fear fell upon him.

But the angel said unto him, Fear not, Zacharias: for thy prayer is heard; and thy wife Elisabeth shall bear thee a son, and thou shalt call his name John.

And thou shalt have joy and gladness; and many shall rejoice at his birth. For he shall be great in the sight of the Lord, and shall drink neither wine nor strong drink; and he shall be filled with the Holy Ghost, even from his mother's womb.

Luke 1:11-15

Zacharias and his wife, Elisabeth, had prayed for a son for years. Then God sent His angel to tell them their prayer was heard and would be answered. God gave this message for Zacharias: "Rejoice because your prayer is heard and your wife is going to bear a child!" Yet Zacharias didn't believe.

Notice how Zacharias responded to this good news:

> **And Zacharias said unto the angel, Whereby shall I know this? for I am an old man, and my wife well stricken in years.**
>
> Luke 1:18

In other words Zacharias was saying, "How do I know you're telling me the truth? How can I be sure you're not lying to me?"

> **And the angel answering said unto him, I am Gabriel, that stands in the presence of God; and am sent to speak unto thee, and to shew thee these glad tidings.**
>
> **And, behold, thou shalt be dumb, and not able to speak, until the day that these things shall be performed, because thou believest not my words, which shall be fulfilled in their season.**
>
> Luke 1:19,20

Zacharias had provoked an angel —not just any angel, but Gabriel, the Angel of the Lord!

I am convinced that angels are assigned to see that the prophecies given in the Word of God come to pass. Psalm 103 says the angels excel in strength and do His commandments. Angels do not have the right to choose their own words. They must speak what God tells them to speak.

When the Word of the Lord came to Gabriel concerning Zacharias, he was quick to relay the good news. But Zacharias, in a mild form, provoked Gabriel with his unbelieving words. Gabriel knew unless he could stop Zacharias from speaking doubt and unbelief, it would not come to pass. So Zacharias was struck dumb for nine months. The angel knew the power that a man's words carry, so he acted in order to prevent Zacharias' words of doubt from interfering with God's plan.

It would be better for some businessmen if they were struck dumb for three or four weeks while they are working on an important business deal. A few wrong words of unbelief can destroy what their angel has been putting together for months!

The words you speak are important. As someone so aptly stated, Samson took the jawbone of a donkey and slew a thousand men—there have been ten thousand business deals killed with the same weapon!

Anytime you speak out of line with God's Word, you're subject to provoking an angel. Jesus said you are going to be justified or condemned by your words. That doesn't mean you will be sent to hell because of your words, but you can lose your eternal rewards because of them. Your words set the cornerstones of your life. In some instances those words are the very thing that assign the angels their job. Watch your words! They're powerful!

Angel Appears to Mary

In Luke 1 the angel Gabriel appeared to Mary.

And the angel said unto her, Fear not, Mary: for thou hast found favour with God.

And, behold, thou shalt conceive in thy womb, and bring forth a son, and shalt call his name JESUS.

He shall be great, and shall be called the Son of the Highest: and the Lord God shall

give unto him the throne of his father David:
and he shall reign over the house of Jacob for
ever; and of his kingdom there shall be no end.

Then said Mary unto the angel, How shall
this be, seeing I know not a man? (Her
question was perfectly legal. Notice she didn't
doubt what the angel was telling her. She just
wanted to know how it was possible.)

And the angel answered and said unto her,
The Holy Ghost shall come upon thee, and the
power of the Highest shall overshadow thee:
therefore also that holy thing which shall be
born of thee shall be called the Son of God.

And Mary said, *Behold the handmaid of the
Lord; be it unto me according to thy word.* And
the angel departed from her.

Luke 1:30-35,38

Gabriel spoke the words which God gave him
to speak, and Mary received those words. She
didn't provoke her angel! She said, "Behold, the
handmaid of the Lord." *Behold* means "look." In
other words, she was saying, "Look! You have
found the woman who will believe You. Be it
done to me according to Your Word."

Mary received what the angel said, and that word was steadfast. It came to pass just as he said it would. Mary conceived that word in her spirit, and it manifested in her physical body. The Bible says the Word was made flesh. It was a twofold action: biological and spiritual.

Mary received the Word of God that came by the angel into her human spirit, then she spoke it with her mouth. Through an act of the God kind of faith, she went to Elisabeth's house and said, "God has done great things for me." She spoke in the past tense. It was already done!

She conceived the Word of God. It was manifested in her physical body.

God's Word took upon itself flesh and was born into the earth. The embryo in Mary's womb was the Word of God!

That was God's Word to Mary. There will never be another to conceive a child that way, but this same principle will work in other situations of life. Believers who will receive God's Word concerning healing into their spirit can experience a manifestation of that healing in their physical body.

The Word of God says you are *delivered from the power of darkness and translated into the kingdom of God's dear Son*. The Word says that *by Jesus' stripes, you were healed*. The Word says *you have been redeemed from the curse of the law*.

If you will receive that Word into your spirit, *it will manifest itself in your body*. That Word of God will become flesh in your physical body.

This same principle applies in the area of financial prosperity. God's Word says He will supply all your need according to His riches in glory by Christ Jesus. (Phil. 4:19.) Luke 6:38 says when you give, it shall be given unto you. When that Word is received into your spirit and allowed to take root there, it will bring forth fruit in your physical life. You will prosper and be in health, even as your soul prospers.

9
Releasing Angels

God's Word is His will. Man is created in the image of God and in His likeness. Therefore, the angels take man's word as being man's will. (Prov. 16:1.)

Abraham Released an Angel

In Genesis, chapter 24, verses 1,4-7, Abraham called on the ministry of an angel.

> And Abraham was old, and well stricken in age: and the Lord had blessed Abraham in all things.

> But thou shalt go unto my country, and to my kindred, and take a wife unto my son Isaac.

> And the servant said unto him, Peradventure the woman will not be willing to follow me unto this land: must I needs bring thy son again unto the land from whence thou camest?

> And Abraham said unto him, Beware thou that bring not my son thither again.

> The Lord God of heaven, which took me
> from my father's house, and from the land of
> my kindred, and which spake unto me, and
> that sware unto me, saying, Unto thy seed will
> I give this land; *he shall send his angel before*
> *thee,* and thou shalt take a wife unto my son
> from thence.

Abraham knew angels would get involved in what he was doing. He said boldly and confidently, "The Lord God shall send His angel before thee."

When the servant found Rebekah, he told her people what Abraham had said:

> The Lord, before whom I walk, *will send*
> *his angel with thee, and prosper thy way;* and
> thou shalt take a wife for my son of my
> kindred, and of my father's house.

> Genesis 24:40

What made Abraham think God would send His angel? How did he know the Lord would do that?

The answer is simple: Abraham knew he had a covenant with God. He knew his covenant rights. He knew where he stood with God!

The most exciting thing about this is that you have the same deal Abraham had, only better! Most people have not prospered in their way because they have spoken against what their angel was doing. They have spoken contrary to God's Word.

Angels listen to what you say daily. If you speak contrary to the Word of God, they are unable to work in your behalf. They will not be obedient to what you say because they hearken to the voice of God's Word. (Ps. 103:20.) If you don't have God's Word in your mouth, if you are not speaking in agreement with it, then your words will not give them any assignment.

Without your cooperation, the angels are hindered. Your words of unbelief bind the angels. Jesus said, "I'll give you the keys of the Kingdom. Whatever you bind on earth will be bound in heaven. Whatever you loose on earth will be loosed in heaven." (Matt. 16:19.) The power of binding and loosing is held by the believer here on earth. That power operates through words. You can bind your angels by just a few words of unbelief! But on the other hand, by speaking God's Word, you can loose the angels to bring that Word to pass in your life.

When you speak in agreement with God's Word, the angels will go before you and prosper your way. They will prosper your way in every area of life—spiritually, physically, financially.

Angels will work for you if you will turn them loose by putting the Word of God in your mouth.

Quit prophesying failure. Start prophesying success by acknowledging the presence of God's angelic forces in your life. Confess: "The angels go before me. They direct me and prosper my way."

When you begin speaking words of faith, you will notice a vast improvement in the affairs of your life.

Abraham set the angel into motion by the words that he spoke. His words caused that angel to go, and things happened just exactly as he said they would. "The mouth of a righteous man is a well of life..." (Prov. 10:11).

Elisha Released the Angels

In 2 Kings 6:8-17, we find an incident in the life of the prophet Elisha when he released angels.

Then the king of Syria warred against Israel, and took counsel with his servants, saying, In such and such a place shall be my camp. And the man of God sent unto the king of Israel, saying, Beware that thou pass not such a place; for thither the Syrians are come down.

And the king of Israel sent to the place which the man of God told him and warned him of, and saved himself there, not once nor twice.

Therefore the heart of the king of Syria was sore troubled for this thing; and he called his servants, and said unto them, Will ye not shew me which of us is for the king of Israel?

And one of his servants said, None, my lord, O king: but Elisha, the prophet that is in Israel, telleth the king of Israel the words that thou speakest in thy bedchamber.

And he said, Go and spy where he is, that I may send and fetch him. And it was told him, saying, Behold, he is in Dothan. Therefore sent he thither horses, and chariots, and a great

host: and they came by night, and compassed
the city about.

And when the servant of the man of God
was risen early, and gone forth, behold, an host
compassed the city both with horses and
chariots. And his servant said unto him, Alas,
my master! how shall we do?

And he answered, Fear not: *for they that be
with us are more than they that be with them.*

And Elisha prayed, and said, Lord, I pray
thee, open his eyes, that he may see. And the
Lord opened the eyes of the young man; and he
saw: and, behold, *the mountain was full of
horses and chariots of fire round about Elisha.*

Elisha declared a decree, "Fear not: for they that
be with us are more than they that be with them."

What do you suppose that servant thought
when Elisha said that? He probably shook his
head and said to himself, "What in the world is
this man talking about? I can plainly see
thousands of soldiers, chariots, and horses
surrounding us. How can Elisha say there are
more with us than there are with them?"

But Elisha prayed, "Lord, I pray thee, open his eyes, that he may see." When the Lord opened his eyes, the young man saw that the mountain was full of horses and chariots of fire!

Who was manning those chariots of fire? The angels, the same ministering spirits that have been sent forth to minister for the heirs of salvation. *And of the angels he saith, Who maketh his angels spirits, and his ministers a flame of fire* (Heb. 1:7).

God provided supernatural deliverance because of the words Elisha spoke. He could have provoked the angels by words of doubt and unbelief, but he didn't. The angels came because of his words: "Fear not; there are more with us than with them."

This incident is one to which God's people should take heed. When we see the problems and the evil things in the world, our heads want to scream out, "What are we going to do? Why did God allow this?"

The angelic host of God is listening, waiting for the go-ahead. But they can't move when they hear God's people say, "What are we going to do? We'll never make it!" But they wait patiently for our words to assign them a task. It is time for the Body of Christ to wake up to the fact that we have legions of angels waiting to move in our behalf.

Calling Angels Off the Job

When you speak things that are contrary to the Word of God, you call your angels off the job. For instance, the Bible says in Psalm 1:3, "Whatsoever he doeth will prosper. He's like a tree planted by the rivers of water." But if you go around saying, "Nothing I ever do works out for good. I always do the wrong thing," your words call the angels off the job.

You can speak words that open the door to the devil and provoke angels. Sometimes people pray the most beautiful prayer of protection over their children. They say, "Lord, watch over them and keep them." Then they turn around and prophesy to the child, "If you play in the street, you will get run over!" Your angel may say, "I don't know why they want this child run over." The angel considers your word to be your will. He will allow what your words allow. The angel may sit there on the curb and watch the child run in front of a car. He listened to your words, and considered them to be your will.

Uncontrolled talk can bring tragedy to your home needlessly. Foolish words and foolish prayers open the door to the devil and invite all kinds of trouble. Jesus put it this way:

> **By thy words thou shalt be justified, and by thy words thou shalt be condemned.**
>
> Matthew 12:37

The angels hearken unto the voice of God's Word. When your words agree with God's Word, you release angels to go and accomplish what was spoken. You may not say *exactly* what God said, but let your words agree with His.

For example, Jesus said, "If you give, it will be given unto you good measure, pressed down, shaken together, and running over." (Luke 6:38.)

Psalm 1:3 says that whatever you do will prosper. When you speak as though those things are true, you will be speaking *parallel* with God.

When you say, "Nothing I ever do works out," you are *perpendicular* with God. That kind of talk will call your angels off the job. They will let the deal you have been working on for months fall through. It doesn't matter to them whether it succeeds or fails. They take your words as being your will.

> **Keep thy foot when thou goest to the house of God, and be more ready to hear, than to give the sacrifice of fools: for they consider not that they do evil.**
>
> **Be not rash with thy mouth, and let not thine heart be hasty to utter any thing before God: for God is in heaven, and thou upon earth: therefore let thy words be few.**
>
> Ecclesiastes 5:1,2

Keep your foot when you go into the house of God. In other words, *don't get your foot in your mouth while you're praying!*

**Suffer not thy mouth to cause thy flesh to
sin; neither say thou before the ange,l that it
was an error: wherefore should God be angry at
thy voice, and destroy the work of thine hands?**

Ecclesiastes 5:6

In other words, *"Don't talk that way before
your angel."*

Have you ever said, "I knew I should never
have started this job. I knew it was too good to
be true. None of these things ever work out for
me"? Don't talk that way before your angel lest
God be angry with your voice and allow the work
of your hands to be destroyed.

"Suffer not thy mouth to cause thy flesh to
sin." You can create all kinds of desires by the
words of your mouth. It's not what goes into the
mouth that defiles the man, but what comes out
of it. (Matt. 15:11.) Some of the desires and
habits of the physical body come because of the
words we speak.

If you've been saying for twenty-five years, "I
just can't eat a meal without pie! I just love
sweets. I guess I'll get as big as a barn," then you

probably will! You've created that desire with your words.

But you can reverse that situation by saying: "I don't desire to eat so much that I become overweight. In the name of Jesus, I proclaim that my body is the temple of the Holy Ghost. Body, you settle down and come into line with the Word of God, in Jesus' name."

Releasing Your Angels

It's time you begin to undo some of the things you've done with your words. It's time to get your words in line with God's Word and release your angels. This prayer will begin that process:

Father, in the name of Jesus, I repent of my ignorance of the Word of God. I ask You to forgive me of the foolish things I've prayed.

In Jesus' name, I bind every word that has released the devil or drawn his weapons toward me. I bind every hindering force that I've ever given strength to by the words of my mouth. I break the power of those spiritual forces, in Jesus' name.

Father, in the name of Jesus, I ask You to guide me in wisdom and understanding through the scriptural methods to set in motion all that's good, pure, perfect, lovely, and of good report.

I covenant with You to pray accurately. I will keep my mouth. I will speak only that which glorifies God. I will let no corrupt communication proceed out of my mouth, but that which is good to edify and minister grace to the hearer. I will not grieve the Holy Spirit of God whereby I'm sealed to the day of redemption, but I will give glory and honor and praise to the Lord Jesus Christ for all that shall be done.

I thank You, Father, that I am the Body of Christ. The enemy has no power over me.

I proclaim that all that is good, all that is blessed of God, all that is in the perfect will of God, all that God has designed for me shall come to me, in Jesus' name.

All of the evil and the bad reports, all that the enemy has designed to deceive me, to lead me astray, to destroy me, my home, or my finances shall be stopped with the name of Jesus and the words of my mouth.

I'm blessed in the city and blessed in the field. I'm blessed in the baskets and blessed in the store. I'm blessed coming in; I'm blessed going out. I'm the head and not the tail. I'm above and not beneath. I'm blessed of Almighty God, strengthened with all might according to Your glorious power.

The Greater One is in me; He puts me over in life. The Spirit of Truth is in me; He gives me divine wisdom, divine direction, divine understanding of every situation and every circumstance of life. I have the wisdom of God.

I thank You, Father, that I'm led by the Spirit of God. I have the mind of Christ and the wisdom of God is within me. In Jesus' name. Amen!

Now, rejoice! You've just released your ministering angels to go to work and accomplish God's Word for your life. You've given them the "green light" to bring you into the Promised Land—that place God has prepared especially for you!

10
Judging the Angels

In 1 Corinthians 6:3, the apostle Paul asks an interesting question: "Know ye not that we shall judge angels?" The saints are going to judge angels.

What angels will we judge?

It can't be fallen angels. Jude 6 says, "The angels which kept not their first estate, but left their own habitation, he (God) hath reserved in everlasting chains under darkness unto the judgment of the great day." The fallen angels already know their fate. They know there is a time coming.

So which angels will we judge?

Every person has at least one guardian angel assigned to him. I believe each of us will judge our angel on this account: Did he do right concerning me on the earth?

Some of you have been mad at your angel because things haven't been working out right.

Examine yourself, and you will probably find that you have provoked him. When you say things that don't agree with God's Word, you provoke your angel.

Many times your words are the problem. You say things like: "Well, this deal will probably be just like all the others. Just at the last minute, something always happens to stop the whole deal."

By grumbling and complaining, you call your angel from his assignment. You have provoked him, and you will have what you **say!**

I'm convinced that the angels we will judge are our personal angels. We will judge the angels that have ministered for us to see whether they did a good job.

I know of one individual who said he fired his angel after somebody broke into his house. Some people won't even lock their homes. They say, "My angels are watching over it." Now, there is no need to overwork your angels. They will do things you can't do, but don't put everything off on them! If you could have locked your house, but didn't, and somebody stole your furniture, shame on *you,* not your angel!

The angels are here to minister for you the things you can't do. They aren't here to cook for you or overhaul the transmission on your car. If they did, you would want them to change the plugs and overhaul the motor. They do things you can't do. When you can lock your house, lock it. Don't go around commanding angels to do things that are your responsibility.

I will share with you a tragic situation that happened several years ago. A man and his wife were killed in a car wreck. Everyone wondered why it happened. He was such a good man. Months after the funeral, someone just happened to mention that the man said, "We have prayed that we will die together."

Don't get the idea that their angel killed them. He just stood there and let it happen.

Let's consider this hypothetical situation: Some guy, twenty-nine years old, gets killed in a car wreck. He makes it to heaven, but is a little put out with the whole deal. When time comes for him to judge his angel, the conversation will probably go something like this:

"Now, guardian angel, I want to know why you allowed me to get killed at twenty-nine years of age. Where were you?"

"I was right there with you in the car."

"Well, why didn't you stop it?"

"Listen to your words: 'I'll tell you, that old car is crazy! Right in the middle of an intersection, it coughed and died. I almost got hit by an eighteen-wheeler! You watch and see, *that thing will be the death of me yet!* It will probably fall to pieces before we get it paid for.' You said that over and over. Then one day a drunk driver ran a stoplight, and your car fell to pieces all over the road!"

Angels are, more or less, spiritual machines. It doesn't make any difference to them when you go to heaven. You can assign them things to do by your words, or you can call them off of their assignment. The Word of God says they hearken to the voice of God's Word and they hearken to men. Jesus said, *"If you confess Me or My Word before men, I'll confess you before the angels of God."* (Luke 12:8.) In other words, if you will say what God said, you will get an audience with angels.

I heard one guy say, "Well, I better go on home because the way my luck is running, I'll probably get run over by a freight train." He didn't get run over by a freight train just because he said that once. But if he keeps saying it, his angel will believe that's what he wants to happen. You may pick up the newspaper one day and read where he was run over by the 9:23 freight. His angel was sitting right there with him until the train came along. Then the angel just got out. If that's the way he wants to go, it doesn't matter to his angel.

Parents have said to their children, "If you play in the street, you will get run over by a car." The angel doesn't know if that's right or wrong. He doesn't dispute your words.

This explains why many tragedies happen. **Wrong speaking and wrong praying provokes angels.**

A husband and wife have a disagreement about buying a new car. He wants it; she doesn't. She says, "You watch and see—you'll get laid off! Then we won't have the money to make the payments—and the note is due on this house at the end of the year. We'll lose our house, sure as the world!"

Now, just stop and ask this question: What is she doing? She is calling things that are not as though they were, but she is doing it on the negative side—using the principle in the wrong direction.

The Scriptures say if a man will believe and not doubt in his heart, he will have whatsoever he says. This principle runs throughout the Bible— Old Testament and New Testament. God told Joshua, "Don't let my Word depart out of your mouth." In other words keep it in your mouth. When you **keep God's Word in your mouth,** you will get an audience with angels.

"Then thou shalt make thy way prosperous, then thou shalt have good success." Angels will be listening to what you say. They will help make your way prosperous.

Even when we call things that are not as though they were on the negative side, it will work. For most people it will work faster than if they were working on the positive side. They say, "Why is it that when I make a negative statement, it comes to pass almost overnight? When I make good confessions, it seems to take weeks and months to come to pass."

It's very simple. They are more highly developed in fear than they are in faith.

Let the Word of God stay in your mouth. Faith comes by hearing the Word of God. Now that being true, where do you suppose fear comes from? Hearing the words of the devil. The more highly developed you get in fear or faith, the quicker the manifestation of what you are saying and believing will come to pass. As Jesus said, by your words you will be justified, by your words you will be condemned. Your words are going to be judged.

There will be people in heaven saying, "But, Lord, I couldn't help it. I couldn't give to this missionary because I never had any money. Every time I got a job I lost it."

The Lord is going to say, *"That was your trouble on earth. You kept saying what you had,* and I said you could have what you said. If you believe and doubt not in your heart, believe what you say and it will come to pass."

Too many Christians don't have faith in what they're saying on the positive side, but lots of faith in the negative. They say so many foolish and negative things that they can't release any faith in positive things.

You must believe that the things you say will come to pass. **Your words assign angels.** You either assign angels things to do, or call them off the assignment by your words. Jesus says whatever you bind on earth will be bound, whatever you loose on earth will be loosed. So it's not God's responsibility at all; it's *your* responsibility.

Yes, we will judge our angels.

11
Angels — A Part of Our Deliverance

Notice the latter part of 2 Kings 6:17. As Elisha's servant looked, "the mountain was full of horses and *chariots of fire* round about Elisha."

In Psalm 68:17-19, there is another passage that talks about chariots.

> The chariots of God are twenty thousand, even thousands of angels: the Lord is among them, as is Sinai, in the holy place.

> Thou hast ascended on high, thou hast led captivity captive: thou hast received gifts for men; yea, for the rebellious also, that the Lord God might dwell among them.

> Blessed be the Lord, who daily loadeth us with benefits, even the God of our salvation.

You could say it this way:"...even the God of our *deliverance.*" **The ministry of angels, the supernatural deliverance that comes to us by angels, is part of the salvation God has provided.**

The word *salvation* means "deliverance, preservation, healing, and soundness." It doesn't just mean to be saved, or to miss hell and make it to heaven. It means super-natural deliverance.

"Blessed be the Lord, who daily loadeth us with benefits, even the God of our salvation." In other words, He loads us with benefits, even the deliverance that comes by the ministry of angels.

Now, the chariots of God are "twenty thousand, even thousands of angels." According to the number of angels given in Revelation, if half of the people on earth were born again and the angels were distributed evenly among us, there would be more than twenty thousand angels per person.

Habakkuk 3:8 gives more light on this subject:

> **Was the Lord displeased against the rivers? was thine anger against the rivers? was thy wrath against the sea, that thou didst ride upon thine horses and thy *chariots of salvation?***

There is that phrase again: *chariots of salvation*. God rides on chariots of salvation or deliverance. Chariots of fire surrounded Elisha. God's chariots are twenty thousand, even thousands of angels. **God rides upon chariots of salvation!**

Supernatural deliverance is available to you today through the ministering spirits of God. Not only did the angels deliver from armies supernaturally, they ministered wisdom, direction, and guidance to the children of Israel.

Angel Brought Light and Darkness

Throughout the Book of Exodus, there were tremendous miracles of deliverance brought about by angels.

> **And the angel of God, which went before the camp of Israel, removed and went behind them; and the pillar of the cloud went from before their face, and stood behind them:**
>
> **And it came between the camp of the Egyptians and the camp of Israel; and it was a cloud and darkness to them, but it gave light by night to these: so that the one came not near the other all the night.**
>
> Exodus 14:19,20

The angel of God caused a cloud to appear that was dark on one side and light on the other. It gave light to the children of Israel and caused darkness to fall on the Egyptians. This is symbolic—a type of what is happening in the end time. *The revelation of God's Word that is coming forth today will be light to the children of God, but darkness to those who walk in darkness.*

Right now you may be thinking: "I sure could use some of those chariots of fire, some supernatural understanding and wisdom."

Remember Exodus 23:20? I'll paraphrase it: "I have dispatched an angel to you to keep you in the way and lead you to the place that I've prepared. But don't provoke him for he will not pardon your transgressions."

Israel had supernatural deliverance given to them. Supernatural guidance. God sent a special angel to lead them, but they did not cooperate with the angel. They missed it; they didn't obey God, His Word, or the angel. Those people from age twenty and older died in the wilderness.

God told Israel, "If you don't hearken to the direction of the angel, he won't forgive you." He was not talking about forgiving their sins because angels do not have the ability or the right to forgive sins. He was talking about not letting them off for the things they spoke against God. Whenever you speak contrary to God's Word, you are subject to provoking the angels.

Therefore we ought to give the more earnest heed to the things we have heard, lest at any time we should let them slip.

Hebrews 2:1

12
Angels in the Old Testament

In 2 Kings, chapter 7, we find an interesting turn of events. Elisha, the prophet of God, had prophesied that there would be no rain. Samaria had been beseiged. There was no food.

The king said, "Go get that prophet because he's the one who caused it."

When the king's messenger got there, the prophet Elisha said to him, "Thus saith the Lord, By this time tomorrow there will be plenty of food in Samaria." Elisha even told him what it would sell for.

An army surrounded the place and had all the food supply cut off. The king's right-hand man said, "Why, if God were to open the windows of heaven, could that happen?"

Elisha said, "You'll see it with your eyes, but you'll never eat of it."

There are four lepers sitting at the gate thinking, "We're gonna die if we sit here! Even if we could get inside the city, the people there are starving to death. We couldn't get anything to eat in there."

Then one of them got an idea. He said, "Why don't we go down to the enemy's camp? They have plenty to eat there. The most they could do is kill us. So what? We're going to die anyway! We don't have anything to lose."

So they started off to the enemy's camp. That's all God was waiting on—for someone to make a move toward the enemy's camp. Nobody else would do it.

Along the way they found shoes, coats, and other things that people had thrown away. Then they realized that everyone had left the camp. The enemy had run off.

Let's pick up the story in 2 Kings 7:5-7:

> And they rose up in the twilight, to go unto the camp of the Syrians: and when they were come to the uttermost part of the camp of Syria, behold, there was no man there.

> **For the Lord had made the host of the Syrians to hear a *noise of chariots,* and a *noise of horses, even the noise of a great host:* and they said one to another, Lo, the king of Israel hath hired against us the kings of the Hittites, and the kings of the Egyptians, to come upon us.**

> **Wherefore they arose and fled in the twilight, and left their tents, and their horses, and their asses, even the camp as it was, and fled for their life.**

Notice, God caused them to hear the noise of chariots.

Remember when Elisha said, "There are more with us than there are with them?" He prayed that God would open the young man's eyes. When his eyes were opened, he saw the hills full of chariots of fire. Well, there's no doubt about it—those chariots were manned by angels because it says, "His ministers are as a flame of fire." As Psalm 68:17 says, "God's chariots are twenty thousand, even thousands of angels."

Because those four lepers dared to go toward the enemy camp, God caused the enemy to hear the noise of chariots and a great host. Those four lepers took over the whole camp, buried the silver and gold, and had plenty of food.

God is just waiting for someone to start toward the enemy's camp. You will get supernatural help when you start toward the enemy's camp. I want you to get this picture because it's prophetic. This is a parallel to the Church today. The Church has been sitting around their gates with people starving inside. All God is waiting on is for somebody to make a move toward the enemy's camp!

King's Right-Hand Man Provokes Angel

And the people went out, and spoiled the tents of the Syrians. So a measure of fine flour was sold for a shekel, and two measures of barley for a shekel, according to the word of the Lord.

And the king appointed the lord on whose hand he leaned to have the charge of the gate: and the people trode upon him in the gate, and he died, as the man of God had said, who spake when the king came down to him.

2 Kings 7:16,17

The king's right-hand man spoke against what God said through the prophet. Because he provoked God and His angels, he died before he could eat of the abundance.

Sennacherib Provoked Angels

Second Chronicles 32:6,7,17,18,21, records another tragic story of provoking angels. Sennacherib had come against Hezekiah, king of Judah, with a great army. Let's pick up the story in verse 6:

> And he set captains of war over the people, and gathered them together to him in the street of the gate of the city, and spake comfortably to them, saying,

> Be strong and courageous, be not afraid nor dismayed for the king of Assyria, nor for all the multitude that is with him: for there be more with us than with him...

> He wrote also letters to rail on the Lord God of Israel, and to speak against him, saying, As the gods of the nations of other lands have not delivered their people out of mine hand, so shall not the God of Hezekiah deliver his people out of mine hand.

> Then they cried with a loud voice in the Jews' speech unto the people of Jerusalem that were on the wall, to affright them, and to trouble them; that they might take the city...
>
> And the Lord sent an angel, which cut off all the mighty men of valour, and the leaders and captains in the camp of the king of Assyria. So he returned with shame of face to his own land. And when he was come into the house of his god, they that came forth of his own bowels slew him there with the sword.

The angel of the Lord slew 185,000 men. (Isa. 37:36.) He wiped out the whole camp, the whole army, in one night. Why? Sennacherib provoked the angel of the Lord.

Balaam Provoked God and Angel

In the Book of Numbers, chapter 22, you find the story of the prophet Balaam. Balak sent for him to curse Israel. Balaam went to God in prayer, and God said, "Don't go because you will not curse Israel—I'm going to bless Israel."

Balak kept after him with promises of fame and fortune. We pick up the story in verse 17:

> **For I will promote thee unto very great honour, and I will do whatsoever thou sayest unto me: come therefore, I pray thee, curse me this people...**
>
> **Now therefore, I pray you, tarry ye also here this night, that I may know what the Lord will say unto me more....**
>
> **And God came unto Balaam at night, and said unto him, If the men come to call thee, rise up, and go with them; but yet the word which I shall say unto thee, that shalt thou do.**
>
> **And Balaam rose up in the morning, and saddled his ass, and went with the princes of Moab.**
>
> **And God's anger was kindled because he went: and the angel of the Lord stood in the way for an adversary against him. Now he was riding upon his ass, and his two servants were with him.**
>
> **And the ass saw the angel of the Lord standing in the way, and his sword drawn in his hand: and the ass turned aside out of the**

way, and went into the field: and Balaam smote the ass, to turn her into the way.

But the angel of the Lord stood in a path of the vineyards, a wall being on this side, and a wall on that side.

And when the ass saw the angel of the Lord, she thrust herself unto the wall, and crushed Balaams's foot against the wall: and he smote her again.

And the angel of the Lord went further, and stood in a narrow place, where was no way to turn either to the right hand or to the left.

And when the ass saw the angel of the Lord, she fell down under Balaam: and Balaam's anger was kindled, and he smote the ass with a staff.

And the Lord opened the mouth of the ass, and she said unto Balaam, What have I done unto thee, that thou has smitten me these three times?

And Balaam said unto the ass, Because thou hast mocked me: I would there were a sword in mine hand, for now would I kill thee.

And the ass said unto Balaam, Am not I thine ass, upon which thou hast ridden ever since I was thine unto this day? was I ever wont to do so unto thee? And he said, Nay.

Then the Lord opened the eyes of Balaam, and he saw the angel of the Lord standing in the way, and his sword drawn in his hand: and he bowed down his head, and fell flat on his face.

And the angel of the Lord said unto him, Wherefore hast thou smitten thine ass these three times? behold, I went out to withstand thee, because thy way is perverse before me:

And the ass saw me, and turned from me these three times: unless she had turned from me, surely now also I had slain thee, and saved her alive.

Numbers 22:17,19-33

Balaam provoked God by going to Him twice when God had already answered him. He provoked the angel to the point of slaying him with a sword.

Three Hebrew Children Released Angel

We find in the Book of Daniel the story of three Hebrew children who were in a bad situation. They had been challenged to fall down and worship before the image that had been made. King Nebuchadnezzar had signed a decree that they had to fall down and worship before the image or go into the fiery furnace. We pick up on this in Daniel 3, verses 15,16:

> ...but if ye worship not, ye shall be cast the same hour into the midst of a burning fiery furnace; and who is that God that shall deliver you out of my hands?
>
> Shadrach, Meshach, and Abednego, answered and said to the king, O Nebuchadnezzar, we are not careful to answer thee in this matter.

To paraphrase that, they said, "Hey, mac, we don't even have to think to answer you. We're not going to worship your image. You can forget it!"

Notice verse 17:

> If it be so, our God whom we serve is able to deliver us from the burning fiery furnace, and he will deliver us out of thine hand, O king.

They said, "Our God is able," but they did not stop there. They affirmed that He would deliver them.

Some have missed the whole point by interpreting this scripture wrongly. They say, "If it be so that our God decides to deliver us, then He will. If not, we'll just burn." *But that's not what this scripture says.*

Let me point out to you why you can't interpret it that way. Verse 17 says, "If it be so..." "If it be so" *what?*

"If it be so that you do what you said you were going to do (throw us in the furnace), then our God is able, and our God will deliver us out of your hand, O king.

"If it be so that you do throw us in the fiery furnace, we're not going to change. If it be so that you throw us in the furnace, our God will deliver us out of your hand."

They decreed a decree: "God will deliver us out of your hand."

Now, look at verse 18:

> But if not, be it known unto thee, O king, that we will not serve thy gods....

It's quite obvious: If God doesn't deliver them, they are not going to serve anybody's god. They're going to be a cinder in about five minutes! They couldn't be saying, "If our God doesn't deliver us, then we want you to know that we won't serve your gods." They were saying, *"If you don't do what you said—if you change your mind and don't throw us in the furnace—we still won't serve your god!"* This is the statement that brought the angel of the Lord on the scene.

The king was furious at what they had said, so he heated the furnace seven times hotter. He used three of the strongest men in the kingdom to throw the three Hebrew children in the furnace. The men that threw them into the furnace died from the heat! But the three young men had supernatural deliverance.

> And these three men, Shadrach, Meshach, and Abednego, fell down bound into the midst of the burning fiery furnace.

> Then Nebuchadnezzar the king was astonished, and rose up in haste, and spake, and said unto his counsellors, Did not we cast three men bound into the midst of the fire?

They answered and said unto the king, True, O king.

He answered and said, Lo, I see four men loose, walking in the midst of the fire, and they have no hurt; and the form of the fourth is like the Son of God.

Daniel 3:23-25

The king looked in and said, "Didn't we throw *three* men in the furnace?"

He said, "Lo, I see *four,* and one is like the Son of God!"

What was different about the fourth man? He was an angel of the Lord. God supernaturally intervened in this situation. Now what caused the angel of the Lord to get involved? Their words of faith.

Then Nebuchadnezzar came near to the mouth of the burning fiery furnace, and spake, and said, Shadrach, Meshach, and Abednego, ye servants of the most high God, come forth, and come hither. Then Shadrach, Meshach, and Abednego, came forth of the midst of the fire.

And the princes, governors, and captains, and the king's counsellors, being gathered together, saw these men, upon whose bodies the fire had no power, nor was an hair of their head singed, neither were their coats changed, nor the smell of fire had passed on them.

Daniel 3:26,27

When they were brought out of the furnace, their clothes were not burned, their hair was not singed, there was no smell of smoke on them.

The king said it had to be the Son of God in there. It was the angel of the Lord. I'm convinced that it was exactly who he said it was: the Lord's personal angel.

The situation that had been set up to destroy them caused them to be promoted in the kingdom. There was supernatural deliverance that came by the ministry of angels.

Then Nebuchadnezzar spake, and said, Blessed be the God of Shadrach, Meshach, and Abednego, *who hath sent his angel,* and delivered his servants that trusted in him, and have changed the king's word, and yielded

their bodies, that they might not serve nor worship any god, except their own God.

Therefore I make a decree, That every people, nation, and language, which speak any thing amiss against the God of Shadrach, Meshach, and Abednego, shall be cut in pieces, and their houses shall be made a dunghill: because there is no other God that can deliver after this sort.

Then the king promoted Shad-rach, Meshach, and Abednego, in the province of Babylon.

Daniel 3:28-30

An angel of the Lord was manifested to deliver the three Hebrew children. They wouldn't bow and they wouldn't burn! Their words summoned the angel of the Lord. Because of supernatural deliverance, they were promoted (made to prosper). The furnace experience was not to make them stronger, but to destroy them. However, the angel of the Lord brought supernatural deliverance **because of their words.**

Faith Releases Angel

Let's look in the sixth chapter of Daniel where Daniel needed supernatural deliverance.

> It pleased Darius to set over the kingdom an hundred and twenty princes, which should be over the whole kingdom;
>
> And over these three presidents; of whom Daniel was first: that the princes might give accounts unto them, and the king should have no damage.
>
> Then this Daniel was preferred above the presidents and princes, because an excellent spirit was in him; and the king thought to set him over the whole realm.

Daniel 6:1-3

The other presidents and princes were jealous of Daniel, so they devised a plan to have him killed. They knew that Daniel prayed three times a day to his God, so they persuaded King Darius to pass a law that anyone found praying to anyone other than the king would be thrown into a den of lions.

> Now when Daniel knew that the writing was signed, he went into his house; and his

windows being open in his chamber toward Jerusalem, he kneeled upon his knees three times a day, and prayed, and gave thanks before his God, as he did aforetime.

Daniel 6:10

Notice Daniel never doubted God's ability or willingness to deliver him from the lions. When it was decreed that they could pray only to the king, Daniel never missed a prayer. He knew that his strength and deliverance came from God.

So the men found Daniel praying and complained to Darius.

Then the king commanded, and they brought Daniel, and cast him into the den of lions. Now the king spake and said unto Daniel, *Thy God whom thou servest continually, he will deliver thee.*

And a stone was brought, and laid upon the mouth of the den...Then the king arose very early in the morning, and went in haste unto the den of lions.

And when he came to the den, he cried with a lamentable voice unto Daniel: and the king spake and said to Daniel, O Daniel,

servant of the living God, is thy God, whom thou servest continually, able to deliver thee from the lions?

Then said Daniel unto the king, O king, live for ever. *My God hath sent his angel,* and hath shut the lions' mouths, that they have not hurt me...

So Daniel was taken up out of the den, and no manner of hurt was found upon him, because he believed in his God.

And the king commanded, and they brought those men which had accused Daniel, and they cast them into the den of lions, them, their children, and their wives; and the lions had the mastery of them, and brake all their bones in pieces or ever they came at the bottom of the den.

Daniel 6:16,17,19-24

There was quite a difference between what happened to Daniel and what happened to the wicked men. Daniel spent the night with the lions; those wicked men didn't last until they reached the bottom of the den!

Then king Darius wrote unto all people, nations, and languages, that dwell in all the earth; Peace be multiplied unto you.

I make a decree, That in every dominion of my kingdom men tremble and fear before the God of Daniel: for he is the living God, and stedfast for ever, and his kingdom that which shall not be destroyed, and his dominion shall be even unto the end.

He delivereth and rescueth, and he worketh signs and wonders in heaven and in earth, who hath delivered Daniel from the power of the lions.

So this Daniel prospered in the reign of Darius, and in the reign of Cyrus the Persian.

Daniel 6:25-28

Daniel Gained Favor

God sent His angel to deliver Daniel from the mouth of the lions because Daniel stood firm in faith. There is a parallel to this story.

According to 1 Peter 5:8, "Your adversary the devil, as a roaring lion, walketh about, seeking whom he may devour." (It doesn't say he *is* a lion; he just acts like one.)

Your angels can shut the lions' mouths! Satan roars a lot, but he is all mouth! Jesus broke his teeth. (Ps. 3:7.) *But some Christians are so soft and pliable that the devil can just gum them to death!* He doesn't need any teeth because they don't have any spiritual backbone.

When you begin to confess God's Word in faith and believe it in your heart, God will minister to your needs; the angels will go to work and bring that Word to pass in your life.

Just as Daniel received favor with the king, God's people will have favor in these last days. We will have favor just as David had favor and as Joseph had favor in the eyes of the pharaoh.

Angel Came Because of Daniel's Words

In the tenth chapter of Daniel, we find another precedent in the Word of God about the operation of angels:

In those days I Daniel was mourning three full weeks. I ate no pleasant bread, neither came flesh nor wine in my mouth, neither did I anoint myself at all, till three whole weeks were fulfilled.

And in the four and twentieth day of the first month, as I was by the side of the great river, which is Hiddekel: then I lifted up mine eyes, and looked, and behold (I saw) a certain man clothed in linen...

And he said unto me, O Daniel, a man greatly beloved, understand the words that I speak unto thee, and stand upright: for unto thee am I now sent. And when he had spoken this word unto me, I stood trembling.

Then said he unto me, Fear not, Daniel: for from the first day that thou didst set thine heart to understand, and to chasten thyself before thy God, thy words were heard, and I am come for thy words.

But the prince of the kingdom of Persia withstood me one and twenty days: but, lo, Michael, one of the chief princes, came to help me; and I remained there with the kings of Persia.

Daniel 10:2-5,11-13

Notice what the angel said: *I am come for thy words*. He didn't come because of Daniel's fasting; he came because of his words.

The words you speak have power with God, and they have power with the angels! The angel came to Daniel to reveal things to him because of what he prayed.

Heard the First Day

Daniel's prayer was heard the first day, but it took twenty-one days for the angel to reach him. Why? Because there was an evil spirit—the prince of the kingdom of Persia—in the atmosphere above the earth who withstood him. He had to call for Michael to come and help him fight his way through.

Again, we find that it was faith-filled words which caused the angel to come on the scene. *Daniel's words released the angel.* Daniel did not have the name of Jesus, but we do under the New Covenant.

...at the name of Jesus every knee should bow, of things in heaven, and things in earth, and things under the earth.

Philippians 2:10

13
Angels in the New Testament

In Acts, chapter 5, the angel of the Lord got involved in a prison break! It seems that the apostles were going about doing signs and wonders among the people in the name of Jesus, and many converts were being added to the Church. This made the high priest and his religious group very indignant.

> Then the high priest rose up, and all they that were with him, (which is the sect of the Sadducees,) and were filled with indignation, and laid their hands on the apostles, and put them in the common prison.
>
> But the angel of the Lord by night opened the prison doors, and brought them forth, and said, Go, stand and speak in the temple to the people all the words of this life.

Acts 5:17-20

The event caused quite a commotion, to say the least! God certainly has a way of delivering His people! These men of God were boldly proclaiming the Word of God among the people, and the angel of the Lord came on the scene.

As God did it for Peter and the other apostles, He will do it today. Angels are still in the ministering business!

Word of Knowledge Delivered by Angel

In the tenth chapter of Acts, we find the account of another angelic visitation:

> There was a certain man in Caesarea called Cornelius, a centurion of the band called the Italian band, a devout man, and one that feared God with all his house, which gave much alms to the people, and prayed to God alway.
>
> He saw in a vision evidently about the ninth hour of the day an angel of God coming in to him, and saying unto him, Cornelius.

And when he looked on him, he was afraid, and said, What is it, Lord?

And he said unto him, *Thy prayers and thine alms are come up for a memorial before God.* And now send men to Joppa, and call for one Simon, whose surname is Peter: He lodgeth with one Simon a tanner, whose house is by the sea side: he shall tell thee what thou oughtest to do.

Acts 10:1-6

Prayer Released Angel

Notice what caused the angel to appear to Cornelius:

Thy prayers and thine alms are come up for a memorial before God.

Again, we find the power of prayer. It will bring the help of angels if necessary. We see it happen here for Cornelius, and we find it also in Acts 12, when Peter was imprisoned:

Prayer Brings Angelic Deliverance

Now about that time Herod the king stretched forth his hands to vex certain of the church. And he killed James the brother of John with the sword. And because he saw it pleased the Jews, he proceeded further to take Peter also.

And when he had apprehended him, he put him in prison, and delivered him to four quaternions of soldiers to keep him; intending after Easter to bring him forth to the people.

Peter therefore was kept in prison: but prayer was made without ceasing of the church unto God for him.

Acts 12:1-5

Peter was in a predicament. He was taken captive and thrust into the inner prison with four quaternions of soldiers (sixteen men) standing guard over him. But prayer was made for him *without ceasing* by the Church.

And when Herod would have brought him forth, the same night Peter was sleeping between two soldiers, bound with two chains: and the keepers before the door kept the prison.

And, behold, the angel of the Lord came upon him, and a light shined in the prison: and *he smote Peter on the side,* and raised him up, saying, Arise up quickly. And his chains fell off from his hands.

And the angel said unto him, Gird thyself, and bind on thy sandals. And so he did. And he saith unto him, Cast thy garment about thee, and follow me.

And he went out, and followed him; and wist not that it was true which was done by the angel; but thought he saw a vision.

When they were past the first and the second ward, they came unto the iron gate that leadeth unto the city; which opened to them of his own accord: and they went out, and passed on through one street; and forthwith the angel departed from him.

Acts 12:6-10

Notice Peter was not worried or fretful. He was sleeping. He had faith that he would be delivered. Though he was to lose his head the next morning, he was sound asleep! His complete faith and trust in God to deliver brought the angel on the scene.

14
My Angels at Work

Everyone has a guardian angel. Jesus spoke of the angels that guard little children. He said, "Their angels do always behold the face of my Father" (Matt. 18:10).

We have just assumed that the guardian angels left us when we grew up; but they haven't. Angels are very much alive and active around us today. They will work in the earth, and they will work for *you!* They will become involved in every area of your life—your home, your business, everything—but only to the extent that you allow them to operate.

We must wake up to the fact that God has provided for us supernaturally. Angels have been sent to do things that we cannot do in our present circumstances. Many times, I have been ministered to in ways that could only have come through the assistance of angels.

> **For he shall give his angels charge over thee, to keep thee in all thy ways. They shall bear thee up in their hands, lest thou dash thy foot against a stone.**
>
> Psalm 91:11,12

I appreciate the ministry of angels. I confess daily that He gives His angels charge over me to keep me in all my ways. I acknowledge their protection and their guidance in my everyday affairs.

There have been numerous occasions when angels have intervened in my life, as well as the lives of my family. They are at work many times and we are not aware of what they are doing for us behind the scene. I want to share some of these experiences with you. It will give you an idea of what angels will do if you would give the more earnest heed to their ministry.

* * * * *

Several years ago, we were flying from England, Arkansas, to minister in the northeastern part of the state. It was rainy, cloudy, and foggy when we took off. We were on an IFR flight plan. When you are flying in bad weather, you depend on your instruments and the controller for directions. The controller, who is tracking you on radar, is the only person in the world who knows where you are and where the other planes are around you.

That day I was in contact with Memphis Center for instructions.

They said, "Climb to 7000."

As we were climbing through the clouds, the Memphis controller came on the radio. "Descend to 6000 immediately!" From the sound of his voice, I knew there was trouble, so it didn't take me long to point the nose down.

My wife said, "What's going on?"

I said, "My angel just tapped that controller on the shoulder and said, 'You dummy! You've got another plane at 7000. Get him down from there!'"

I had no fear at all. I knew that the ministering spirits were taking care of the situation. I had no doubt about it—my angel was at work!

* * * * *

Another time we were landing in Indiana. I was on final approach when suddenly I heard the tower telling another aircraft, "Turn right! You have traffic at 12 o'clock. Turn right immediately!"

I looked out, and there he was—right in the window. Normally, that would be a frightening situation, but it didn't bother me at all. The knowledge of God's promises took the fear out of me. I know the angels have charge over me, and they are keeping me in all my ways.

Angels get involved in emergency situations, but so many times they go unnoticed.

There was the time I was scheduled to speak at a meeting from which I would return home after dark. But the rotating beacon, which must be operating when a plane is flown at night, was not working on my airplane. It had been out for three months, but I had been so busy on my farm that I had not replaced the bulb. I had intended to drive to the meeting, but some situations developed on the farm that delayed my leaving until it was too late to drive. So I had to fly.

I knew the light was out, so I told the Lord since flying was the only way for me to get there on time, I needed Him to do something about it. That night after the meeting when I started the engine on my plane, I turned on the rotating beacon that hadn't worked for three months. It worked perfectly!

* * * * *

Several years ago my daughter, Annette, who wore contact lenses, went out one night to burn the trash. She lost a contact lens in the grass. She came in the house and said, "Daddy, I lost my contact lens."

"Where did you lose it?"

"Out by the trash barrel."

The thought which came to my head was, "Well, we'll never find it. We might as well forget it." But I had been confessing all the good things that God's Word promises: Whatever I do will prosper. No weapon formed against me will prosper. I'm blessed coming in and going out.

I just said, "In the name of Jesus, we'll go find it."

My head said, "You dummy! You know you aren't going to find it."

Though my head knew I wouldn't find it, my inner man acted on my words. Besides that, my angels were standing there. They said, "We had better get busy. He'll be looking all night."

I took the flashlight, and we walked outside to the trash barrel. I flipped on the flashlight and saw something glistening on the grass. I slipped up to it; and sure enough, there balanced on top of a blade of grass was Annette's contact lens!

* * * * *

During a meeting in Corpus Christi, Texas, my wife and I were staying in a motel. I went ahead to the elevator. Peggy was to follow. I waited for a time, then finally she came.

"Where have you been?" I asked.

"The door wouldn't latch. When I pushed on it, it would just come open."

"What did you do?"

"I didn't do anything. I just said, 'Angels, you'll have to take care of it. We have to go.'"

When we came back, we had to use a key to get in. The door was locked. When we were ready to go to the service that night, I decided to fix the door. I did everything—pushed down on it, lifted up on it, slammed it—but never could get it to latch. So I said, "Angels, you'll have to do it again. We have to go." When we returned, we had to use the key to get in. The door was locked.

There is always somebody trying to explain away supernatural things. But these aren't just "things that happen." God wants us to realize that angels are very much involved in our affairs.

Then some people always look for the spectacular and miss the supernatural.

* * * * *

While on a ski trip in Colorado, my daughter, Beverly, and I took some pictures. Beverly loaned those pictures to a girl who had gone with her, and she had them in her car in Tulsa, Oklahoma. She stopped at an intersection and opened the door for some reason. The envelope with the photos fell out into the street, but she drove away not realizing what had happened. The next day another lady who had gone on the ski trip went to her office to work. The pictures were on her desk! When she asked her boss where they came from, he said his wife was out jogging and found them laying in the street. He recognized her in the photos and brought them to her.

What do you suppose the odds are of that happening in Tulsa, Oklahoma? There would be so many zeros behind that you couldn't count them! A small thing, but interesting.

* * * * *

Then there was the time I went to North Carolina to speak. The radar was not working on my airplane; so when we met with storms, we had to be vectored around them by the Center.

I said to my wife, "When we get to Hickory, North Carolina, there will be somebody at that airport who will fix this radar." I released my faith in that statement.

When we landed in Hickory, I tied the airplane down, went inside, and asked if there was somebody who could fix my radar.

The man said, "Radar?! We don't have anybody that works on *radios* much less radar!"

I just went on and didn't say anything more about it. Three days later we flew to Charlotte, North Carolina. There were thunderstorms again that day. When we took off, I reached over and turned on the radar. It worked perfectly, painting those cells all the way to Charlotte!

We didn't get a drop of rain on us all the way to Charlotte. When we left the next day, it was clear. I decided to check out the radar. When I turned it on, it wouldn't work.

Somebody said, "Well, if the angel fixed it, why didn't it stay fixed?"

Angels are not in the habit of doing things that can be done by men, unless it's an emergency. The emergency was over.

When I took it to the shop to be repaired, I said, "Father, in the name of Jesus, I assign an angel to stand by the guy who works on this radar. Show him what's wrong with it and what to do to fix it." That man had worked on it several times before without finding the problem. But this time he found the problem in just a few minutes.

Angels can be involved in situations if you will let them. They want to get involved in your life.

Angels are interested in doing things you can't do. Now, don't send them out to overhaul your car or change a flat tire! That's not their job. Their job is to minister for you.

* * * * *

Another time I was working with three men on my farm, overhauling a small hydraulic pump. We were standing in a gravel driveway around the tailgate of a pick-up truck. While we were working, one of the needle bearings in the pump dropped in the gravel. This needle bearing was about the size of a pencil lead and a sixteenth of an inch long.

After looking for ten minutes, we couldn't find it. The first thought that came to my mind was, "We'll never find it in this gravel. Let's just forget it." But the Spirit of God rose up in me and I remembered the contact lens. We had been looking under our own ability. I realized that I was about to shut out my angels. So I said, "In the name of Jesus, I'm going to find that bearing!"

When I knelt down again, the first thing I saw was that little needle bearing! A coincidence? No! My words brought the angels on the scene to help me find the bearing.

* * * * *

Then there was the time I was driving down the freeway in Dallas, Texas. As I was exiting off the freeway, a car stopped in front of me so I had to stop on the off-ramp. Another car came down the ramp, going about 60 m.p.h., and hit my car in the rear. The gas tank burst and gasoline went everywhere. The car was totalled; but no one was injured.

I remember the sensation I felt at the moment of impact. It seemed as if there were pillows surrounding me. I just floated around inside that car! I wasn't scratched and didn't get one sore muscle. Again, I am convinced that the angels were involved. Afterwards, I remembered Psalm 91:4: **He shall cover thee with his feathers.**

There is no doubt: I was ministered to by angels.

15
Angels Unaware

by Annette Capps

Divine Protection

Psalms 91:5 says, "Thou shalt not be afraid for the terror by night; nor for the arrow that flieth by day" (and what I'm going to share happened at night).

In 1978 I went to minister in Burlington, Colorado. A friend, Pam Johnson, from Tulsa, Oklahoma, went with me.

When we got there a couple of nights before the meeting began, we stayed with a friend who lived on a farm about fifteen miles out of town. Since we didn't have a meeting the next morning, we decided to drive into town to visit some people.

Before we left, I had an urge to pray; so I walked outside into the field and prayed in the

Spirit for forty minutes. I didn't know *why* I was praying — I just knew I was supposed to.

After a while, the girls came out and said, "Come on! Let's go to town."

The three of us got into the front seat of the car and headed to town. We were driving through hilly country, and it was a dark night— no moon, no stars, no other cars on the road. You couldn't see your hand in front of your face.

When we got about halfway to town, we topped a hill, going about 55 or 60 miles per hour. Standing in front of us were some black angus cattle scattered all over the road.

Before we could hit the brakes, **we hit the steers!** I began to say, "Jesus! Jesus!" The girl driving the car was busy holding onto the wheel, but Pam began to pray in the Spirit. It was a most unusual experience!

Though we hit the steers doing 55 or 60 miles per hour, we only slid forward in our seats about two inches! Our heads didn't hit the windshield.

We didn't hit the dashboard. It felt like pillows were all around us, just like we were cushioned!

Confession Brings Protection

By this time in my life, I had learned about the 91st Psalm. For days, weeks, and even years, when I got up in the morning, I would say:

> **Thank You, Father, that I dwell in the secret place of the Most High God. I abide under the shadow of the Almighty Whose power no foe can withstand. No weapon formed against me shall prosper.**

> **A thousand may fall by my side. A thousand people may have car wrecks, but thank You, Father, that You have given Your angels charge over me, and it won't affect me.**

The way to have supernatural deliverance is to believe for it and confess it! This is for every believer. A thousand may fall by your side, but it will not come nigh you!

There are lots of Christians who don't believe it, and some unbelieving believers don't appropriate the promises of God.

I have always heard, "If you have a choice between hitting a big steer or a brick wall, you had better hit the brick wall!"

When we hit, the impact of it crushed the hood into a "V" toward the windshield. The frame of the car was bent so badly that we couldn't get out on the left side of the car. The whole front end was smashed. (I found out later that the car was a total loss!)

You see, I had already been protected for years by saying, "Thank You, Father. You've given Your angels charge over me, and no weapon formed against me shall prosper." Those words which had been set forth in the spirit, protected us at that time.

Out of the Abundance of the Heart

I can imagine what some people would have said at a time like that because as Jesus said, **out of the abundance of the heart the mouth speaks.** When you find yourself in a situation like that, the thoughts that are in your heart will come out of your mouth.

The moment we hit and came to a stop, I said, "Praise God! Hallelujah! Thank You, Jesus!" Those words came so fast out of my innermost being that it was hard for me to believe I said them.

In the air tragedy that happened several years ago in the Virgin Islands, the voice recorder of the plane showed that the captain said, "My God! It's going to kill us all!"

I too could have said something negative about the circumstances if I hadn't been grounded in the Word. My inner man was programmed to protection by supernatural means.

Change the Picture

Even before I found out about Psalm 91, the Holy Spirit had showed me as a child how to protect myself from accidents. I didn't have many accidents, but things would come into my mind. I didn't fall and break an arm, but I would see myself doing it. Or I would see myself cutting my foot by stepping on a piece of glass. Then the

Holy Spirit showed me how to come against that—and I didn't even know about Psalm 91!

I would instantly remove that picture of tragedy from my mind and picture myself being delivered from it. Maybe I would fall, but it wouldn't hurt me. I would instantly run a movie before my eyes and see myself going through the same thing, only this time I wasn't hurt.

It was supernatural deliverance; I had already protected myself. Then when I found out about Psalm 91—that a thousand can fall at my side and ten thousand at my right hand, but it wouldn't come near me—I had double protection because I had programmed and renewed my mind and my heart by agreeing with the Word of God.

Knowing His Name

Psalm 91 says, **"They will call upon Me, and I will answer them and deliver them."** God will deliver people who call upon Him. He will deliver them, He says, "...because they know My name."

Many people don't know the Name of God. There are several names for Him. One name is Jehovah Rapha—the God that healeth thee. There is also the God that delivers thee. These truths will deliver you if you will appropriate them.

Appropriating the Promise

People don't appropriate God's promises. Then when tragedy happens, they wonder **why** God allowed it to happen. It happened because they didn't appropriate the promises of God. They didn't really believe it was for them; they believed it was for someone else. But I experienced it. You can experience it too if you will act on God's Word and believe for these things.

The angels hearken to the voice of God's Word. Just a few hours before the accident happened, I had been voicing God's Word concerning deliverance from evil, trouble, and problems.

Every day I purposely confess Psalm 91. At that particular time in Colorado, I had confessed it obviously by praying in the Spirit. Before we left I had felt impressed to pray in the Spirit, that is, in another language. Even though I didn't know what I was praying about, I must have been speaking the Word of God and interceding about divine protection for this particular incident.

Heed God's Warning

If you only knew, I believe you would find that every time a person has had a catastrophe, *God tried to warn that person*. I know this has happened to me several times. God would try to warn me some way—to have me pray. If you will look back you will find that God tried to warn you of danger as He warned me.

When we hit that steer, it was a powerful impact. Damage to the car was enormous. Though we had not fastened our seat belts (a practice I certainly am not recommending to anyone!), none of us were injured. This was an unusual situation.

All the lights on the car went out, and the car was blocking the road. Immediately I said, "Let's get out of this car right now! It's so dark we have to go to both ends of the road and stop traffic!"

So we took off, two girls in one direction and I in the other direction. As I was running up the road, I was saying, "Oh, God! You've got to help us!"

I knew that if another car came over the hill, the driver wouldn't be able to see our car setting crosswise in the road with its lights out.

As I reached the top of the hill, I turned and looked. The girls had run a good way down the road and had stopped a pickup truck. Then I heard a truck coming up the hill. It sounded like an eighteen wheeler going about 70 miles per hour! That's when I said, "God, You're going to have to do something!"

Someone Fixed the Lights

I could hear the truck coming closer and closer. As I was looking at the shadow of our car in the headlights of the pickup, I saw "someone" walk around to the front where the hood was bent and reach under the hood. Suddenly the headlight came on. Then the dome light came on, lighting up the inside of the car.

When the emergency flashers came on, I thought, "My goodness! Those girls really have it together. They've done something to the battery cable to get the lights to come on! That's brilliant!"

The truck came over the hill. The driver saw the car in time to veer off to the right. He went over halfway into the ditch, but he missed the car!

After the traffic had passed and all the lights were on in the car, I walked back down the hill. The girls were still standing at the pickup truck, talking to the driver. That was a quarter of a mile down the road!

They Thought I Did It

When they came up to the car, I asked, "How did you ever get the dome light and emergency flashers to work? How did you get the battery cable connected again?"

They looked at me and said, "We thought *you* did that! We've been standing here talking to the man in the pickup. We thought *you* did something to the lights."

I didn't do anything to the lights! They didn't do anything to the lights! And we know it wasn't the steers! That's obvious.

This happened eight miles out of town. All around us were farms. One side was a feed lot. No one else was there. But someone had fixed the lights in that car so no one would be hurt. **No doubt that "someone" was a ministering angel!**

Angels of Mercy

In 1974 I went with a group to South America on a missionary crusade. On the way home when our plane got to Atlanta, we were told that there had been severe ice storms in Arkansas and that we would be unable to get home.

We had been gone for a week and were very tired. We were ready for some good home cooking!

About five minutes later as we were sitting there on the plane praying, a voice came over the speaker and said, "Well, folks, something has happened. The airport in Memphis has just been opened. It's been iced over for two days, but now it's open. We're going to Memphis!"

We were supposed to fly into Memphis and have ground transportation to Little Rock. When we landed, we were told, "The airport is open, but the roads are closed."

We kept thinking we would get out of there soon, but it kept snowing and sleeting. More ice!

For sixteen hours we sat in the Memphis airport. All night we slept on our suitcases. There weren't enough seats for everyone. A boat show was being held there, so some of the girls slept in the bottom of the boats!

Prayer, Then Action

I told my friend, Cindy, "I don't believe, that since we prayed and asked God to be able to get back to Arkansas, we should be stuck here in the

Memphis airport. There has to be a way for us to get home! I'm going to call and try to get a bus to Little Rock."

When I called, a man said, "Yes, we have a bus leaving in about twenty minutes."

I hurried back to the group and said, "We're leaving! We're going home!"

The others just laughed and said, "How do you expect to get home? We're stuck here!"

"I just found out that there's a bus going to Little Rock."

"Oh, there's not a bus going to Little Rock! And even if there was, you're liable to get stuck by the side of the road all night and freeze to death!"

"No! We're going to Little Rock on that bus!"

When we gathered up our suitcases and started to leave, we were told, "Once you step out of this airport terminal, we are no longer responsible for you. And we won't try to find you if you get lost!"

"That's fine," I said. Then we headed for the door carrying two large suitcases, two small suitcases, and a large ship that Cindy had bought in South America.

When we stepped out the door, it was a shock to our bodies. For a week we had been in South America where the temperature was about 100°, we were dressed in summer clothes. In Memphis the temperature was about 20° and there were several inches of snow on the ground.

So there we stood in the cold, and we couldn't find a taxi! This was definitely one time when the angels needed to be in charge. We had to have help!

You Have Not If You Ask Not

As we stood there, I said, "Let's just pray and ask God to send someone to help us get to the bus station." So we agreed in prayer.

About that time a van pulled up and about fifteen businessmen with briefcases jumped into it. As we were standing there freezing, one of the men got out and asked, "Where are you going? Why are you standing here in the cold?"

"We're trying to get to the bus station."

Then he said, "I think we can get you in our van. Come on." Their van held about fifteen people uncomfortably, and even more uncomfortably with the two of us, our ship, and four suitcases! But we managed to squeeze in.

The driver dropped the men at their hotel, then headed for the bus station. The minutes were ticking away and it was getting closer to the time the bus was to leave. Finally, we made it.

When we walked into the bus terminal, we saw a crowd of people. They were everywhere, sleeping on floors and across seats. There was a long line at the ticket counter, so we went to the rear and waited.

Discouragement and Wavering Faith

We reached the ticket window about two minutes before the bus was to leave. I was so happy. I knew this was an answer to our prayer. I said, "Two tickets to Little Rock, please."

The man behind the counter looked at me and said, "Lady, we haven't had a bus to Little Rock out of here in two days!"

"But, sir, when I called, someone said there was a bus going to Little Rock at 3:20 this afternoon."

"Lady, I don't know who told you that, but they're crazy! Do you see all these people? Half of them are trying to get to Little Rock. They've been here for two days. That's why they're sleeping on the floors."

What else was there to do? We took our suitcases and found a couple of seats. I was very discouraged at that point and just about let my faith waver over my prayer. But as we were sitting there, I said, *Lord, You have to do something quick. We can't get a bus out of here, and we can't go anywhere else. We need help!*

Help—Just in Time!

We sat there a little longer (with Cindy still holding her ship!), then through the swinging doors walked two men. They were very tall and were wearing overcoats and hats. They walked all around the terminal, stepping over people, then stopped right in front of us. One of them looked at Cindy and said, "Where did you get the ship?"

She said, "South America."

Then he said, "What are you doing here?"

"Well, sir, we're trying to get to Little Rock, Arkansas."

"You are? Why don't you get on the bus out there?"

Then I said, "But, sir, the man at the counter said there's not a bus going to Little Rock."

He looked at me and said, "I happen to have *inside information*. There's a bus loading right now."

Persistence Paid

I ran to the counter and said, "I want two tickets to Little Rock, right now."

"I'm sorry, lady, but there aren't any buses going to Little Rock."

"But I have information that one is leaving now."

So he called and, sure enough, he found that a bus was loading right then. We got our tickets and started for the door, still lugging the two big suitcases, the two little suitcases and Cindy's big ship. As we struggled along, a young man who had been lying on the floor asleep suddenly jumped up and said, "Here! Let me help you!" It was as if someone had slapped him. He grabbed our suitcases and ran out the door to help us on the bus. I'm sure he has no idea why he did that!

The Two Tall Men

As we were waiting to get on the bus, one of the two tall men walked up and said, "Did you get your tickets?"

"Oh, yes. Thank you for helping us, sir. We really do appreciate it!"

"Well," he said, "I just wanted to be sure you made it. I'll see you a little further down the line." Then he turned and walked away.

Cindy and I looked at each other and said, "Wonder what he meant by that?"

Then we saw the other guy. He was standing behind some glass, waving to us. We waved back. Then he did a strange thing: he pointed to himself and acted like he was dialing a telephone, then pointed to us.

I said, "How is he going to call us? He doesn't have our telephone number."

Then he pointed to himself again and acted like he was writing, then pointed to us.

I said, "How is he going to write us a letter? He doesn't have our address. These guys are really nice, but they're strange."

As the bus drove away, I kept thinking about what he had said, "I'll see you a little further on down the line." But we were so excited to be on that bus, we didn't care what happened. We were going home!

The bus stopped about thirty miles from Memphis. As we were sitting there, I looked out the window. There stood the man with the overcoat! "Cindy, look! Where did he come from? He wasn't on the bus." He smiled, waved, and we waved back. We looked at each other again, thinking how unusual it was.

After driving a few more miles down the road, the bus stopped again. This time I was almost afraid to look out the window. When I did glance over, there he was again! He waved, and we waved back.

Then suddenly my lightening fast mind caught it! In sign language, to say messenger, you first make the sign for message, then you make the shape of a person. That makes message a personal noun, messenger. When that man acted like he was writing on a tablet, he was saying message. Then he pointed to himself, meaning messenger.

"Cindy," I gasped, "that's an angel!"

The Word of God says that angels are messengers. God had sent two angels to supernaturally get us on the bus.

Then as we headed down the road, I began to see things along the way that looked familiar. So I walked to the front of the bus and said, "Excuse me, sir. Does this bus go through England, Arkansas?"

"Yes, it sure does."

"Then would you please stop and let us off when we get there?"

That bus let us off on the corner of the main street in my hometown!

Now, what does the Bible say about angels? The Bible says, "Are they not all ministering spirits, sent forth to minister for them who shall be heirs of salvation?" (Heb. 1:14).

God didn't send those angels so that I could say, "I saw one!" He sent them because we were in a moment of need.

I have the utmost confidence that God will provide supernatural help for us in any problem, difficulty, or need, wherever we are on earth; and if necessary, God will send legions of angels to help.

Angels are real. They are sent to minister for us!

16
Let Your Angels Work for You!

Bless ye the Lord, all ye his hosts; ye ministers of his, that do his pleasure.

Psalm 103:21

One thing that gives pleasure to the Lord is found in Psalm 35:27:

Let them shout for joy, and be glad, that favour my righteous cause: yea, let them say continually, Let the Lord be magnified, which hath pleasure in the prosperity of his servant.

According to this scripture, God takes pleasure in the prosperity of His servants. Well, if He takes pleasure in the prosperity of His *servants,* don't you think He would take even more pleasure in the prosperity of His *sons?* Galatians 4:7 says we are not servants; *we are sons,* joint-heirs with Jesus. It gives God pleasure when we prosper.

Some people think God wants us to always have problems and be in lack in this life. But if God takes pleasure in the prosperity of His people and it is the angels' job to do God's pleasure, then they must prosper people! Remember Abraham's words to his servant: "The angels will go before you and prosper your way."

The angels will help us if we believe in them and speak words of faith. Psalm 107:2 says, "Let the redeemed of the Lord say so, whom he hath redeemed from the hand of the enemy." But many would not dare say so. In other words, speak what God says about the situations of life.

The angel of the Lord encampeth round about them that fear him, and delivereth them.

Psalm 34:7

When the angel of the Lord encamps round about you to deliver you, then you will be delivered!

How do you release the angels? How do you get them involved so that they minister for you? Predominantly in two ways:

1. **Keep God's Word in your mouth.**

2. **Pray.** Jesus said He could pray and get more than 72,000 angels. They are available to you as well.

Take Psalm 91 and make it personal. Read and confess it this way:

I dwell in the secret place of the Most High. Therefore, I shall abide under the shadow of the Almighty.

I will say of the Lord, *He is my refuge and my fortress:* my God; in him will I trust. Surely he shall deliver *me* from the snare of the fowler and from the noisome pestilence. He shall cover *me* with his feathers, and under his wings shall I trust: his truth shall be *my* shield and buckler.

I shall not be afraid for the terror by night; nor for the arrow that flies by day; nor for the pestilence that walks in darkness; nor for the destruction that wastes at noonday.

A thousand shall fall at *my* side, and ten thousand at *my* right hand; but it shall not come nigh *me.*

Only with *my* eyes shall I behold and see the reward of the wicked.

Because I have made the Lord, which is my refuge, even the most High, my habitation; there shall no evil befall *me*, neither shall any plague come nigh *my* dwelling.

For he shall give his angels charge over *me*, to keep *me* in all *my* ways. They shall bear me up in their hands, lest I dash *my* foot against a stone.

I shall tread upon the lion and adder: the young lion and the dragon shall I trample under *my* feet.

These verses of Scripture describe the person who places his trust, confidence, and faith in the Most High God. But not only does he dwell in that secret place and abide under that shadow, he also says something: *I will say of the Lord, He is my refuge and my fortress: my God; in him will I trust.* This psalm should be the bold confession of every child of God.

Some may say, "I know someone who tried that, but it didn't work for them!" There are probably more people that it does not work for than those that it does work for. But that doesn't change the Word of God. "A thousand may fall at *my* side, and ten thousand at *my* right hand; but it shall not come nigh me."

The last three verses of Psalm 91 are spoken from God toward us:

> **Because he hath set his love upon me,** *therefore will I deliver him: I will set him on high, because he hath known my name.*
>
> Psalm 91:14

What is God's name?

He is *El Shaddai*—the Almighty God, the All-Sufficient One, the God Who is more than enough!

He is *Jehovah-Rapha*, the Lord God that healeth thee.

He is *Jehovah-Jireh,* the Lord God that supplies.

So many don't know God's name. If they don't know these are His names, how can they call upon Him for these things?

> **He shall call upon me, and I will answer him: I will be with him in trouble;** *I will deliver him,* **and honour him.**

> **With long life will I satisfy him, and shew**
> **him my salvation.**
>
> Psalm 91:15,16

Our God will show us salvation—deliverance, preservation, healing, and soundness.

The ministry of angels is part of the salvation (deliverance) that God has given us. How shall we escape if we neglect so great salvation that comes by the ministry of angels?

Put the angels to work by keeping God's Word in your mouth.

Give His Word a voice—*your angels are listening!*

Charles Capps is a retired farmer, land developer and ordained minister who travels throughout the United States sharing the truth of God's Word. He  has taught Bible seminars for over thirty years sharing how Christians can apply the Word to the circumstances of life and live victoriously.

In the mid '90s the Lord gave Charles an assignment to teach end-time events and a revelation of the coming of the Lord.

Besides authoring several books, including the best selling *The Tongue, A Creative Force*, and the minibook *God's Creative Power*®, which has sold over 4 million copies, Charles Capps Ministries has a national daily syndicated radio broadcast and weekly TV broadcast called "Concepts of Faith".

Annette Capps is an ordained minister, businesswoman and licensed airplane pilot. A lifelong student of the Bible, her curiosity led her to investigate the similarities of "quantum physics" and the teachings of Jesus Christ. This powerful combination  opened new dimensions for those seeking a bridge between the Bible and modern science.

Building on her former teaching subjects such as *The Mind-Body Connection*, and *Changing the Course of Your Life*, she demonstrates the practical application of spiritual principles in everyday life.

Guest appearances on the Concepts of Faith television program with her father, author and teacher, Charles Capps have generated extraordinary interest as have radio interviews and magazine articles. In addition to the book, *Quantum Faith*, Annette has authored four other books entitled; *Reverse the Curse in Your Body and Emotions*, *Understanding Persecution*, *Angels* and *God's Creative Power® for Finances*.

Annette resides in Tulsa, Oklahoma where she is the President of Annette Capps Ministries and acting Executive Director of Capps Publishing and Charles Capps Ministries, Inc.

For a complete list of CDs, DVDs, and books by Charles Capps, or to receive his publication, Concepts of Faith, write:

Charles Capps Ministries
P.O. Box 69, England, Arkansas 72046
Toll Free Order Line (24 hours)
1-877-396-9400
www.charlescapps.com

BOOKS BY CHARLES CAPPS AND ANNETTE CAPPS

Angels

God's Creative Power® for Finances

God's Creative Power® - Gift Edition
(Also available in Spanish)

BOOKS BY ANNETTE CAPPS

Quantum Faith®

Reverse The Curse in Your Body and Emotions

Understanding Persecution

BOOKS BY CHARLES CAPPS

Triumph Over The Enemy

When Jesus Prays Through You

The Tongue – A Creative Force

Releasing the Ability of God Through Prayer

End Time Events

Your Spiritual Authority

Changing the Seen and Shaping The Unseen

Faith That Will Not Change

Faith and Confession

God's Creative Power® Will Work For You
(Also available in Spanish)

God's Creative Power® For Healing
(Also available in Spanish)

Success Motivation Through the Word

God's Image of You

Seedtime and Harvest
(Also available in Spanish)

Hope - A Partner To Faith

(Also available in Spanish)

How You Can Avoid Tragedy

Kicking Over Sacred Cows

The Substance of Things

The Light of Life in the Spirit of Man

Faith That Will Work For You

Powerful Teaching From Charles Capps

If you have enjoyed reading this book, you can find more dynamic teaching from Charles Capps in these revolutionary books.

Can Your Faith Fail?

Faith That Will Not Change

Have you ever stepped out in faith only to later feel that you have failed? If you are like most Christians, at some point in your life, you have questioned the word God gave you. The truth, however, is that faith is a law and God's laws always work. This is a practical guide to encourage you in your walk with God. It will teach you how to put your faith into action to produce results in your life.

ISBN-13: 978-0-9819574-6-3

You Can Change
The Direction of Your Life

How You Can Avoid Tragedy
And Live A Better Life

How often have you heard the question: "They were such good Christians! Why did this happen to them?" Many believers' lives have been overwhelmed needlessly by defeat and tragedy.

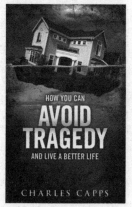

Satan's greatest weapon has been deception – getting you to believe something contrary to God's Word. Wrong speaking, wrong praying, and wrong believing will destroy your faith. Praying "If it be Thy Will," has opened doors for the devil's opportunity when God's Will is already revealed in His Word.

ISBN-13: 978-0-9819574-5-6

Understanding Paul's
"Thorn In The Flesh"
And How You Can Overcome
The Messenger Of Satan Assigned To You

Triumph Over The Enemy

In Second Corinthians 12:7, Paul writes about "a thorn in the flesh, the messenger of Satan" who had been sent to harass him. This "messenger" was sent to create problems and stir up the people against Paul everywhere he preached. But Paul knew the key to overcoming this obstacle – he learned to exercise his God-given authority here on the earth!

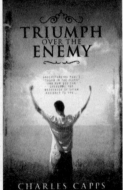

This book will show you how to walk in God's grace and triumph over this enemy sent to harass and keep you from God's greater blessings in your life.

ISBN-13: 978-0-9819574-2-5